TEMPORAL CODES FOR MEMORIES:
Issues and Problems

JOHN M. MacEACHRAN MEMORIAL
LECTURE SERIES, 1976

Sponsored by
The Department of Psychology
The University of Alberta
with the support of
The Alma Mater Fund of the University of Alberta
in memory of John M. MacEachran,
pioneer in Canadian psychology

TEMPORAL CODES FOR MEMORIES:
Issues and Problems

BENTON J. UNDERWOOD
NORTHWESTERN UNIVERSITY

 LAWRENCE ERLBAUM ASSOCIATES, PUBLISHERS

1977   Hillsdale, New Jersey

DISTRIBUTED BY THE HALSTED PRESS DIVISION OF

JOHN WILEY & SONS

New York   Toronto   London   Sydney

Lawrence Erlbaum Associates, Inc., Publishers
62 Maria Drive
Hillsdale, New Jersey 07642

Distributed solely by Halsted Press Division
John Wiley & Sons, Inc., New York

Library of Congress Cataloging in Publication Data

Underwood, Benton J   1915-
    Temporal codes for memories.

    Bibliography: p.
    1. Memory.   2. Human information processing.
3. Time—Psychological aspects.   I. Title.
BF371.U5   153.1'2   77-1954
ISBN 0-470-99115-1

Printed in the United States of America

Contents

Preface

This book represents an expanded version of the material covered in the MacEachran Lectures given at the University of Alberta in March, 1976. I can only hope that my excursion into the temporal coding of memories as recorded in this book justifies the high honor I felt at being asked to participate in this annual lecture series.

It is a pleasure to acknowledge again the continued and critical support by the Psychological Sciences Division of the Office of Naval Research in carrying out the experiments reported here. The current support is authorized by Contract Number N00014-76-C-0270.

The data-collection phase of the first major experiment to be reported began in 1971. During the past five years the direct supervision of my laboratory has been handled in succession by three dedicated and patient graduate research assistants, Joel Zimmerman, Charles Reichardt, and Robert Malmi. The latter assistant gracefully accepted my unrealistic timetable for completion of experiments during the six-month period before the lectures were to be given and proceeded to see that the deadlines were met. I am grateful to another assistant, Susan Kapelak, for the data of Experiment 3, which was collected as a part of another project. Finally, my thanks are given to Phyllis Van Hooser for her careful preparation of the final manuscript.

B. J. U.
Evanston, Illinois

TEMPORAL CODES FOR MEMORIES:
Issues and Problems

1
The Problem

The human mind encompasses an enormous number of memories. Whether all memories that were ever established still persist is a matter for coffee debates; the fact remains that the usual adult possesses an amount of information in memory that essentially defies measurement. Represented among these memories are those reflecting experiences that occurred at definite points in time. A chronicle of these memories would in one sense constitute the history of the individual. A chronicle implies an ordering of events that corresponds with true ordering. Major events in our lives, such as eighth grade graduation, high school graduation, marriage, and retirement, would be ordered properly because there is a necessary order to such events. But when we ask about memories that are less inevitably ordered, we begin to be less certain of the chronicle. Did your father lose his job before or after your second child was born? Did you become a member of the bowling team before or after you remodeled your kitchen? When we ask such questions, we begin to see that many events that are well remembered seem to have, at best, only a crude location in the chronicle of our experiences.

The problem of central interest in this book is the nature of the temporal coding of memories. Just how this became a problem of moment will be detailed later. It is sufficient at this point to indicate that our attempts to solve certain problems of memory functioning led me to believe that differences in temporal coding of memories were implicated. We were thus led to undertake some experimental work to supplement evidence available in the literature; the intent was to get at least a preliminary understanding of the variables that govern our ability, or lack of it, to distinguish by memory the ordering of events in time.

It seems to me that most of the evidence available, as well as evidence that arises from introspection, leads to a conclusion that our ability to identify points in time at which particular memories were established is very poorly developed. One wonders why evolutionary changes (purported to have occurred over the centuries as

1

adaptive changes) have not given us memories that are in some way intrinsically dated. Why has nature treated us so uncharitably? Had there been an ageless observer at the sparkling moment of the creation of the egg—or of the hen—we would be no better off than we are today, for I am sure the observer would have soon forgotten which came first.

It might be presumed by some that, because our ability to date memories is so poorly developed, such abilities are of little consequence for our welfare. Or, without implying a cause: Of what importance is the ability to order memories correctly? Of what importance is it to remember that the kitchen was remodeled before the time a bowling team was formed? Our legal system depends heavily upon an external dating system (a calendar system) to establish an order of events that can be accepted by all. At the same time, it seems beyond a doubt that justice may not have been served in many, many cases where the order of events was determined by the testimony of a witness. If a decision concerning the guilt or innocence of a citizen charged with murder depended upon the memory of a witness as to whether he had heard a gunshot before or after he heard the squealing of automobile tires, I would be uncomfortable with the decision. A recent newspaper story told of a disagreement between the Internal Revenue Service and a businessman over the deductions he had taken in calculating his income tax. These deductions were for business expenses, expenses which consisted primarily of costs for luncheons and dinners for his clients. Many of the witnesses testified under oath that they had indeed been recipients of the luncheons and dinners, but when the Internal Revenue Service asked them for specific dates they were quite unable to reconstruct the dates. It has been reported (Gibson & Levin, 1975) that children afflicted with dyslexia are particularly inadequate in their memory for the temporal ordering of events.

The above is merely to suggest that our inability to tie our memories for events to certain points in time, and thereby to order the events accurately, is not without impact on our lives. Still, we are able, within some margin of error, to associate our memories with their times of formation, and the question is how we are capable of such dating at all.

In the first two chapters, I will establish the contours of the problem as I see them. For the initial step, I will report three rather diverse studies as a means of illustrating procedures and data that are said to deal with temporal coding.

EXPERIMENT 1

We brought together 24 brief statements describing events that had occurred from 1968 to 1975. Pretesting indicated that most college students would remember that these events had indeed occurred, although it is not definite that the memories for them were established at the time of their occurrence. The descriptions of the 24 events, along with the month and year of occurrence, are given in Table 1. They are divided into three groups of eight each (three forms) for reasons which will become clear momentarily. In Table 1 the events are listed in order from most recent to least recent, although on the test sheet given to the subjects the statements were randomized. Each subject supplied a date for only 8 of the 24 events, and the subgroups of 8 events each are identified as "forms."

Students in a large, advanced undergraduate lecture course served as subjects, all being tested simultaneously. The eight statements were printed on a single sheet. After each statement, two blanks occurred: one identified as "year," the other as "month." The three forms were interlaced before distribution to the subjects, so we assume that the three subgroups were equivalent in their knowledge of the events. The instructions at the top of each sheet were as follows:

> Below are listed eight events that have occurred in relatively recent years. The events were so momentous and were so widely reported by TV, radio, and newspapers that most college students will remember that the events did indeed happen. Our interest is with your memory concerning *when* each event happened. There is some belief among those who study memory phenomena that our knowledge of the position of an event in the flow of events is relatively poor. In fact, however, there is very little systematic evidence on the matter. This "test" is an attempt to get preliminary evidence on the accuracy of our memory for the placement of events in time.

TABLE 1

Descriptions of the 24 Events for Which Subjects Were Asked to Supply
a Date of Occurrence (Month and Year) in Experiment 1

Description of events	Date of occurrence
Form 1	
James R. Hoffa reported missing	7/75
The tidal-basin incident involving Wilbur Mills	10/74
Richard Nixon resigned the presidency	8/74
Billie Jean King defeated Bobby Riggs in tennis	9/73
Governor George Wallace shot	5/72
Attica (New York) prison riot	9/71
The tragic incident at Chappaquiddick Island involving Ted Kennedy	7/69
Martin Luther King assasinated	4/68
Form 2	
The *Apollo-Soyuz* linkup in space	7/75
Hank Aaron established a new home-run record	4/74
Patty Hearst kidnapped	2/74
Spiro T. Agnew resigned the vice presidency	10/73
President Nixon visited mainland China	2/72
Kent State students killed	5/70
The first man stepped on the moon	7/69
Robert Kennedy shot	6/68
Form 3	
Death of Aristotle Onassis	3/75
Evel Knievel failed in his attempt to rocket across the Snake River Canyon	9/74
Alexander Solzhenitsyn exiled from Russia	2/74
Former President Lyndon B. Johnson died	1/73
Baseball star Robert Clemente killed in plane crash	12/72
Disney World in Florida opened	10/71
Former President Eisenhower died	3/69
U.S.S. *Pueblo* captured by North Koreans	1/68

Note: Each subject was given eight statements, thus there were three forms.

> We would like you to give your best guess as to the year and month during which each of the eight events occurred. You may find this difficult, but please fill in each blank—the year and the month—for each event, even if you feel that your estimates are more or less guesses.

The subjects also entered their ages. The test was unpaced, with most subjects finishing within five minutes.

Some blanks were left unfilled by some subjects. These test sheets were discarded. In addition, all subjects 23 years of age and over were eliminated. Other sheets were discarded randomly to equalize the groups (forms) at 36 subjects each. The data to be presented were based on 108 subjects, with the number of subjects in the five age groups of 18, 19, 20, 21, and 22 years being 6, 30, 46, 21, and 5, respectively.

The subjects made an estimate of the month and year for each of the events. The test was given to the subjects in November 1975. Therefore, as a metric, the true age of an event was calculated in months backward from November 1975. Thus, the event concerning James R. Hoffa was 4 months removed from November 1975, the Wilbur Mills incident 13 months removed, and so on, until the oldest event on Form 1 (the assassination of Martin Luther King) was 91 months removed from the point in time at which the subjects made their judgments. The dates given by the subjects were likewise transformed into months removed from November 1975. A mean for these scores for each event was determined to get an estimate of group accuracy. The plot in Figure 1 shows the outcome, with the diagonal line indicating the true number of months by which the events were removed from November 1975.

Although the collective judgments could probably not be used to replace a calendar, the correspondence between the true number of months removed and judged number of months is quite high, the product—moment correlation being .96 for the 24 events. Other evidence might lead to the expectation that events close in time would be judged to have occurred further back in time than was actually true and events very remote in time would be judged to have occurred at times less remote than was true. As can be seen in Figure 1, there is at best only a suggestion of this in the data. It has been

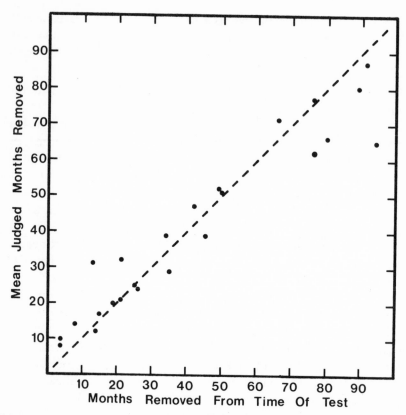

FIGURE 1. Mean judged months removed (from November, 1975) for 24 events, differing in number of months removed. The diagonal line represents perfect correspondence between age of events and judged age (Experiment 1).

reported (Linton, 1975) that errors in estimates increase in magnitude as the memory gets older. Statistically, this would mean that the standard deviation of the judgments would increase the further back the event occurred. This was generally true, but there were many exceptions for particular events.

We next asked about the relative ordering of the events by the individual subject. The true orderings were correlated with the ordering inferred from the eight dates assigned the events for each subject. The mean of these correlations was .79, and all 108 were positive. The lowest correlation observed was .08, but only 2 of the

108 subjects ordered the events perfectly. A hit may be defined as assigning the correct month and year for an event. The hits averaged just under one (.98), and 45 of the subjects had no hits. In terms of events, the maximum number of hits was 50 percent ("Nixon resigned the presidency"), but no hits were observed for three of the events. The average error by which the subjects missed was 15.01 months, with a range of from 1.38 months (approximately 40 days) to 35.38 months (just under three years).

Decades of psychophysical research would lead to the expectation that, the closer two events were in time, the greater the likelihood that the two events would be misordered in time. For each form, the number of errors made by each subject in ordering was determined for all combinations of two events. Thus, if the subject assigned an older date to "Hoffa reported missing" than to "the King-Riggs tennis match," it was counted as an error. For each form, 28 such comparisons could be made, or 84 across the three forms. These 84 combinations were grouped according to the time separating the two events, each group spanning 10 months, so that nine groups covered the entire range. For the two-event combinations falling within each grouping, the percent error was determined, and these values have been plotted in Figure 2. Expectations were fully realized; the greater the time separating the two events, the less the likelihood of a misordering of those two events. Even with the shortest separation (1–10 months), the judgments were somewhat better than anticipated if the subjects were merely guessing.

If the separation between two events was kept constant but the absolute age of the events varied, it would be expected that errors would increase as age increased. The present data lacked a sufficient number of events to make this determination. However, Squire, Chace, and Slater (1975) have demonstrated the relationship. Their subjects were asked to choose the most recently aired television program that had been aired for only one season between 1962 and 1973. The difference in the age of the programs presented for all choices was five years. The number of errors increased as the age of the programs presented for choice increased.

In our experiment, when the subjects were first given the task, there was much moaning and groaning as to the absurdity of the

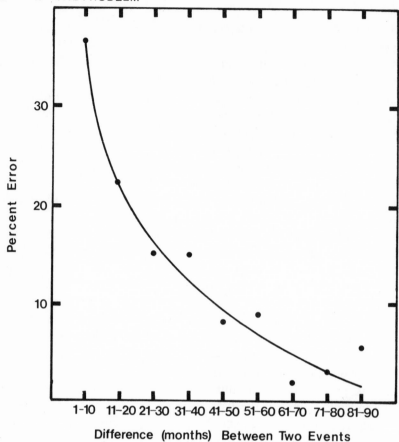

FIGURE 2.   Errors in ordering two events as a function of the separation of the two events in time (Experiment 1).

request to supply dates for the events. After complying with the request, there were many comments about the difficulty of the task, how it was necessary to guess, and how poor "my memory" was. Still, the results have shown that the subjects were able to supply dates that were meaningful, either when combined, or when examined for each subject independently. True, many of the errors were very gross, and only 2 subjects of the 108 tested were able to supply dates that correctly ordered all eight events. But that some information was available to most subjects for making educated guesses seems undeniable.

EXPERIMENT 2

The events of interest in Experiment 1 were events that might be called momentous; they were of varying durations, but even those that were momentary were extended in time by aftermaths and by the reporting of the news media. In Experiment 2 we turned to a sharply contrasting set of events, events that had only a brief duration, and the entire series of events had a very short time span. Furthermore, the events were quite homogeneous in character and utterly lacking in newsworthiness. The subjects in Experiment 1 were, in spite of their moaning, intrigued with the task given them. The subjects in Experiment 2 merely moaned. They were shown 32 words in succession for three seconds each, and then were asked to make recency judgments for pairs of words: Which one of these two words occurred most recently in the list?

Each subject was presented four successive lists of 32 words each. After the presentation of each list, 12 recency judgments were requested, that is, 12 pairs of words were presented and the subject was requested to choose (by circling) the most recently presented word in each pair. Furthermore, each recency judgment was followed by a lag judgment in which the subject circled a number from 0 through 14 to indicate the number of words believed to have separated the two words in the list. For each list there were three pairs having true lags of 0, 1, 5, and 10 words. Thus, across the four lists there were 12 tests for each lag. The tests were unpaced. The words occupying positions 1, 2, 15, 21, 22, 30, 31, and 32 were not tested.

The subject was fully instructed about the nature of the test requirements before being presented the first list. The 128 words used in the four lists consisted of a random sample from a larger pool of 315 four-letter words drawn randomly from the Thorndike—Lorge (1944) tables. The words were assigned randomly to lists and to positions within the lists, and all subjects were given the four lists in the same order. A total of 96 college students was tested.

The subjects in this experiment might have justifiably moaned; both decisions (choosing the most recently presented word and estimating the number of words separating the two) proved to be very difficult. Some of the subjects did not score above chance in

choosing the most recent word. The results for both response measures are shown in Figure 3. The upper panel gives the percentage of
correct responses (correct recency decisions); the lower panel, the
mean lag judgments, both as a function of lag. Although in an
absolute sense the discrimination is quite poor, that there is a lag
slope for both response measures seems unmistakable. A test of the
four points in the upper panel indicated reliability, $F(3, 285) = 7.10$,
$p < .01$, as did the test for the lower panel, $(F = 112.67)$. It will be
noted that the number of correct decisions is a little better at zero
lag than at a lag of one. Although this difference was not reliable
statistically, it will be argued later that even the small difference
may have psychological meaning. The lower panel shows that the lag
judgments for short lags were overestimated, those for long lags,
underestimated. As noted earlier, this has been a fairly universal
finding

It is conceptually possible to view the two response measures
(number correct and lag estimates) as being independent. This
would imply that a subject might know that two events were widely
separated in time but not know which occurred most recently. Two
lines of evidence indicate, however, that this was not true. Since
each subject had four lists, reliability measures were calculated by
combining the results for Lists 1 and 2 and correlating the performance measures with those for Lists 3 and 4 combined. The reliability
was not high. For correct responses, the product—moment correlation
was .39. While this value is reliably higher than zero, it is certainly
not very useful for predicting individual performance. To evaluate
the reliability of the lag judgments, a slope measure was derived.
This was calculated for each subject as the sum of the judgments for
lags 0 and 1 divided by the sum of the judgments for lags 5 and 10.
A ratio of one would indicate no discrimination (no slope), with
discrimination increasing as the ratio decreases below one. The
reliability of this measure was .29. Finally, the correlation between
the slope measure and the correct-response measure (for all four
lists) was .36. This indicates that a subject who had a large number
of correct responses also tended to have a steeper lag function than
did a subject with a small number of correct responses.

If recency judgments and lag judgments are positively related, it
should follow that, when an incorrect recency judgment is made,

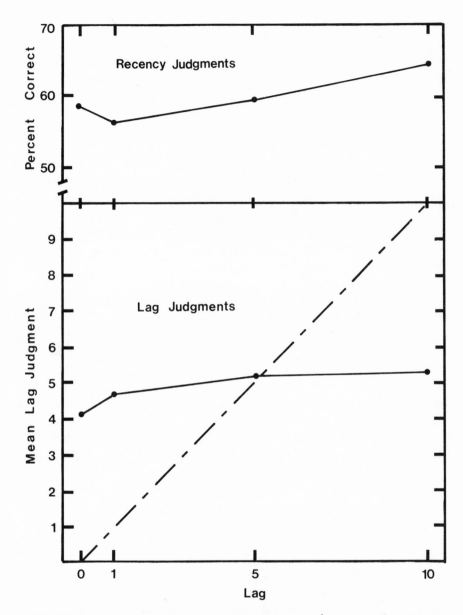

FIGURE 3. Percentage of correct recency judgments (upper panel) and mean lag judgments (lower panel) as related to lag. The diagonal line in the lower panel represents perfect correspondence between lag and judged lag (Experiment 2).

11

the corresponding lag judgment should be more in error than that given following a correct recency judgment. All subjects had at least one incorrect recency judgment at each lag. It was possible, therefore, to determine a lag function for incorrect and correct recency judgments without loss of subjects. Of course, pairs for which incorrect responses were given were, in some way, more difficult than pairs for which correct recency judgments were given, although certainly some correct responses resulted from guessing. In any event, the lag judgments for incorrect recency judgments showed absolutely zero slope, all four points being at approximately a mean of five. Thus, when subjects made errors in the recency judgments they made lag judgments of five on the average, and this was independent of the true lag. As may be seen in Figure 3, the mean lag judgment combined across lags is approximately five. The data apparently indicate that when subjects do not know which member of the pair was most recent, they choose a lag near the means of their other lag judgments—a central-tendency effect. These data indicate, as did the correlational evidence, that accuracy in lag estimates is modestly related to correctness of recency judgments.

That subjects will show a central-tendency effect in lag judgments when they are incorrect in their recency judgments is a curious finding. In Figure 2 it was shown that the closer together two events are in time, the greater the likelihood that an error would be made in a recency judgment. It might be expected that subjects would have learned this relationship in their various experiences. That is, it might be expected that their judgments would reflect this correlation between error likelihood and the closeness of two events in time. Therefore, when a pair is given for which they have no "feeling" as to which member of the pair was most recent, they should conclude that the two must have been close together in the list and thereby be led to assign a very short lag estimate. Clearly, this was not the case in the present data, and since similar outcomes have been reported in other studies (e.g., Brelsford, Freund, & Rundus, 1967; Hintzman, Summers & Block, 1975), it seems to be reliable.

One other finding should be noted: Performance did not improve across the four lists. Whatever skill underlies the correct choice of the most recently presented word was not developed within the relatively short period of practice given the subjects.

EXPERIMENT 3

Experiment 2 involved homogeneous events (words) within a larger event (list of words). Recency judgments for events of this type will be spoken of as within-task or within-list judgments. These are to be contrasted with judgments that follow the presentation of two or more tasks or lists, following which the subject is asked to identify the list membership of the elements or units making up the separate tasks. These will be called between-task temporal judgments, and such judgments were required in Experiment 3.

The procedures involved were very simple. The 100 college-student subjects were given three successive lists of 20 words each for study following explicit instructions concerning the nature of the test to be given. On the test, the 60 words were printed in random order on a sheet of paper. After each word the numbers 1, 2, and 3 appeared, and the subject was asked to circle the number representing the list in which the word had occurred. The words were all four-letter words. They were exposed for 2 seconds on the study trial, and 2 minutes were allowed to complete the test. After the test was given on the first three lists, the entire procedure was repeated with another set of three lists of new words. Because the performances on the two sets of lists were highly comparable, the judgments have been combined for the sets. The product—moment correlation between the number of errors made on the first set of three lists and the number made on the second set for the 100 subjects was .67.

The results are plotted in Figure 4, in terms of the percent of the words in each list that were assigned list membership in each list. For example, of the words in List 1, 55% were correctly assigned as having occurred in List 1. Of the remainder, 30% were assigned to List 2, 15% to List 3. It is apparent that correct assignments are greater than would be expected by chance (33%), but, in any absolute sense, performance is poor when it is seen that the correct responses were only slightly above 50%. However, the nature of the errors indicate some temporal information that is not given in the correct-response measure. The clearest case involves List 1, where it is seen that when an error is made it is more likely to involve assigning the word to List 2 than to List 3. The data for this list

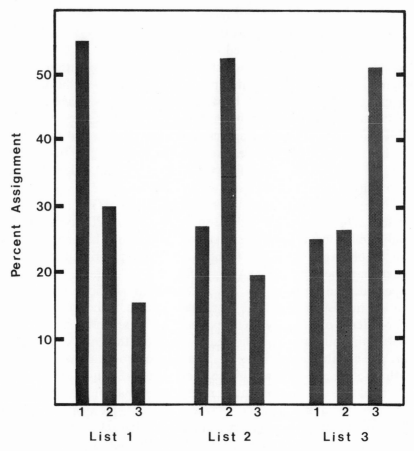

FIGURE 4.   The percent of items in each list that were assigned to each list. The three tallest bars represent correct assignments, the others incorrect assignments (Experiment 3).

could be described as reflecting a temporal generalization gradient. This effect was less clear for Lists 2 and 3. For List 2, one might expect symmetry in the two error sources (Lists 1 and 3) and a larger difference between the two error sources when List 3 items were involved. It would appear that there was a response bias, so that when in doubt the word was assigned to List 1. The source of this bias is not evident. It might suggest that the subject applied some reasonable notions: "If I can't remember where this word occurred. . .," or "If I don't recognize this word as having occurred at all, it must have been in the first list. Otherwise, I would have remembered it." It was noted earlier that the subject did not seem to apply such logic to the within-list judgments of lag in Experiment 2, but perhaps the principle was more readily available to the subjects in Experiment 3 because of its simplicity or directness. Such a principle of determining judgments could have also inflated the number of correct responses for List 1. Based on a simple forgetting notion, the number of correct responses should have increased across the three lists when in fact the number decreased slightly.

THE RECENCY PRINCIPLE

Three sets of data have been examined as an introduction to the type of phenomena with which I will be dealing. The data from these experiments were presented primarily for demonstration purposes. They were not very analytical with regard to the possible types of information that entered into the judgments made by the subjects. For example, in Experiment 3, if subjects did not recognize a test word as having been in any of the study lists, it may have seemed somewhat incongruous to ask them to make judgments of list membership.

The data from the three demonstration experiments have been interpreted at a general level as showing the fallibility of the temporal dating of memories. In the present section, I want to turn to a somewhat different area of discourse in order to demonstrate a contrary aspect of behavior. In any type of study involving the relative dating of memories, two temporal intervals must be critical. Assume two target memories, T1 and T2, and a memory test for ordering. First, there is the interval between T1 and T2 (lag). Second, there is the interval between T2 (the most recent of the two events) and the point in time at which the test is given. This second interval is the focus of the discussion in this section. The point to be made is that, when this second interval is minimal in length, our capabilities of distinguishing between the most recent event and previous events is, in most situations, quite extraordinary. As the flow of information into the memory system proceeds over time, it is as if the information we are dealing with at the moment can be protected by a shield or curtain from incursions into it by less recent memories. As time passes and the information changes, the older curtain gradually raises and a new one descends. This recency principle is sometimes said to be mediated by a selector mechanism (Underwood & Schulz, 1960). I will review some of this evidence to illustrate the power of this mechanism.

Subjects learned a paired-associate list consisting of single-digit numbers as stimuli and consonant syllables (each of three letters) of low association value as response terms. Such a list is very difficult to learn, primarily because of the difficulty of integrating or unitizing the three letters of each response term. The performance of 18 subjects given 20 anticipation trials was examined.

The eight consonant syllables were made up of 15 different letters. This means that there was some letter duplication, and it also means that 11 letters of the alphabet were not included. In their attempts to learn this difficult list, the subjects produced many misplaced letters and many sequences of letters that were not involved in any of the syllables. Not including misplaced correct responses (a correct syllable given to a wrong stimulus term), there were 789 letters produced which were wrong, in the sense that they were a part of a wrong sequence, single letter responses, and so on. Of these errors, only 20 (2.5%) were letters that were not included within the eight consonant syllables. Furthermore, because most of these were produced by only a few subjects, and frequently repeated by the subjects, it is quite possible that these errors were preceptual in nature, such as misreading a B for an R. Effectively, the subjects did not import letters; their response attempts were almost exclusively limited to letters that were in the list. A single study trial initially seemed to have limited the pool of letters with high precision.

We studied the errors made in learning a paired-associate list in which 12 different single letters were used as response terms. These lists had two-digit numbers as stimulus terms for the 12 response terms. Actually, two such lists were employed, each being learned by a different group of 18 subjects for 15 trials. In learning one of these lists a total of 427 errors was made, an error being counted as a case when a letter was produced to the wrong stimulus term. Of these 427 errors, only 3% were letters not actually in the list. For the other list, 540 errors were made, of which 4% were letters not actually used as response terms. It should be clear that the letters within the list were not the first 12 letters of the alphabet, nor the last 12, nor was any other principle of selection evident. The 12 letters were randomly chosen from the alphabet. One might think that this would be a highly favorable condition for the subject to give letters that were not in the list; the evidence indicates otherwise, and again, even the small number observed may have been due to reading errors.

In a third study, subjects learned a 16-pair word list with the pairing such as to produce high intralist similarity among instances of concepts. The 30 subjects made a total of 1,424 overt errors, but only one of these errors was a word not present in the list. One subject responded with "yellow" when the correct response was "canary."

These studies indicate that subjects can, after a single study trial, effectively limit their information to the appropriate units; this is done in spite of the fact that those eliminated as inappropriate may often in other circumstances be in a common pool with the appropriate units. Recency of stimulation, even that produced by a single occurrence, seems to set the memory for a unit quite apart from the more remote memories of highly similar units.

In the above cases, recency operates to separate memories for verbal units presented and not presented in a particular situation. However, the recency principle operates with much the same effectiveness when both the appropriate and inappropriate units have been experienced in the same situation. It has been shown many times that in the $A-B$, $A-D$ transfer paradigm, the intrusion of B terms during the learning of $A-D$ pairs is an infrequent occurrence. Again, a single study trial on $A-D$ sets the D terms apart from the B terms, in spite of the fact that commonality exists, because of the use of the common stimulus terms in both lists. Even if some of the B terms are carried over into the second list, intrusions of B terms not carried over are infrequent (e.g., Twedt & Underwood, 1959).

It was noted earlier that the two critical intervals in the memory for the order of events are the T1–T2 interval and the interval between T2 and the test for the order of the two events. In the $A-B, A-D$ paradigm, each list may be considered an event. Hence, the T1–T2 interval between the two lists and the T2–test interval would be considered critical. It was because of puzzling results produced by the manipulation of these two intervals with this paradigm that we were led to a variety of experiments on variables involved in temporal coding. We will turn to these puzzling data in the third chapter. In the remainder of the present chapter, we will be concerned with establishing the background assumptions underlying the work.

ORIENTATION

It is quite common in contemporary work on memory to conceive of a memory for an event as consisting of different types of information. It is my preference to speak of these different types of information as being the attributes of memory (Underwood, 1969a). Thus, the memory for a word may consist of an acoustic attribute, various semantic attributes known collectively as meaning, a modality attribute, and so on, including a temporal attribute. To have a theory about memory is, within this framework, to have a theory about how one or more of the attributes enter into memory functioning—how the attribute(s) enter into performance on memory tests.

Some of the attributes may be viewed as having more or less direct representation in memory. For example, in developing the theory that has come to be known as frequency theory (Ekstrand, Wallace, & Underwood, 1966), it was assumed that one of the mechanisms in memory is a counting mechanism. Each occurrence of an event is "tabulated," and the subject can, when requested, make public the sums. Stated in this manner, the theory is extremely crude on at least two counts. First, the characteristics of the counting mechanism per se may be sharpened. That is, does each occurrence of an event establish an independent trace, or is there a more direct summing mechanism implied by trace strength? Second, it seems likely that an event may produce several different classes of frequency information. A word, for example, may have a frequency representation in memory in terms of the perceptual response (visual, acoustic) made to it. The memory for the event might also carry an independent count of the frequency of a common meaning response which occurs with each presentation. These are not matters of concern for the moment. They are mentioned to indicate that frequency information, however viewed, has a relatively direct representation in memory. The question we ask concerns the temporal attribute: Does it have direct representation in memory?

The manifestation of a direct temporal attribute is implied by ideas about biological clocks or biological calendars. Somehow, an event is given an identification tag that locates its position with respect to the positions of many other events, which occur over time. Such ideas have arisen primarily from the decades of research dealing with the estimation of very short time intervals, a line of research that goes on unabated (Zelkind & Sprug, 1974).

At one time, my belief in the continuity of behavioral principles led me to do a series of studies on the judgment of short temporal intervals, including interference effects in the relatively short-term memory for the duration of two intervals. I had hoped they might produce some firm leads to an understanding of temporal discriminations when lists or items were the events of interest. These data still languish in a file drawer, for I was unable to make a reasonable connection. Another line of contemporary work (e.g., Kornblum, 1973, Section 7) deals with perception of temporal order for two events that occur very close together in time, when closeness is measured in milliseconds. As in the case of the judgment of the duration of short temporal intervals, this work on the ordering of two events, which occur very close together in time, may not be irrelevant to the problems of the temporal coding of memories viewed in a far more extended time period. I simply have not included them in the present work because I have not been able to pull the draw strings together. Also, I have chosen not to work with the temporal attribute as being one that has a direct representation (e.g., a biological clock) in memory. This may be an incorrect decision; it is quite possible that the crispness of the recency principle, as illustrated earlier, would yield to such a notion. However, since my central interest is in the breakdown of the recency principle, I simply reached the decision that the temporal attribute will be viewed initially as a derived attribute. By this is meant that our knowledge of the temporal location of memories is based on other attributes of memory for events, and the central task is that of identifying what these other attributes are and the nature of the role they play.

The perspective on one further issue needs to be made clear. When we do a memory experiment (or an experiment in any other area), the observations open to the public (the experimenter) are two in number. First, the subject is exposed to a given event under the experimenter's control. Second, the subject responds in some way on a memory test. Three questions are frequently asked about the processes or stages that fall between the two public events:

1. Was there storage? Did learning occur?

2. What changes (decay, forgetting) may occur for the stored memories (collection of attributes) over time (before the second public event)?

3. Which attributes mediated performance on the test?

Frequently, these questions are reduced to two: Was a deficit on the memory test due to inadequate storage or to a failure of retrieval? To a greater or lesser degree, most of us have been involved in looking at our data in such a way as to draw conclusions about storage and retrieval. These efforts shade over into other questions, such as whether or not recognition tests involve retrieval mechanisms. In this search for answers, we frequently forget about the stage implied by the second question; and it may well be that we will ultimately conclude that, for the temporal attribute, this stage is critical. There is a further complication, which essentially prevents us from logically reaching conclusions about storage, persistance, and retrieval.

Recent evidence (e.g., Galbraith, 1975b) indicates that attributes that are appropriate for performance on the memory test could be quite available, but the subject does not utilize them. One of the unfortunate consequences is that, because the attributes were not utilized, we may infer that the attributes were not stored. It should be noted that Melton (1963), in his influential article, did not use the word *retrieval* in his description of the third stage or question. Rather, he used the phrase *trace utilization*, which could imply two factors: the availability of appropriate attributes and the choice by the subjects of attributes to mediate their test performances. For example, it has been shown that a simple instruction from the experimenter will cause subjects to choose a particular attribute to mediate verbal-discrimination performance, although another might have been the voluntary choice of an uninstructed subject (Ghatala, Levin, & Subkoviak, 1975). Since subjects may, for whatever reason, instruct themselves on memory tests, this source of variance at the attribute selection level must be recognized. Given that four different factors, each of an unknown quantity, may be involved in the performance on a memory test and that some of the attributes are known to be quite independent of each other, we must recognize the near logical impossibility of identifying the source of a deficit in memory when one occurs. This is regrettable, but may as well be faced. It does not mean, of course, that we will cease speculation about these thoroughly confounded intervening events, but perhaps we will recognize them as speculations.

2
A Preliminary Analysis

The loose focus of this chapter is on certain independent variables, which may be involved in the temporal coding of memories. I will identify variables that have a proven effect on temporal coding, those that will likely have an effect, and those that seem to offer leads for theoretical thinking about the critical attributes that mediate temporal coding. Attention will be directed primarily toward, variables influencing within-list temporal judgments; those influencing between-list judgments will be evaluated in a later chapter.

SERIAL ASSOCIATIONS

In many cases we infer the order of events because we know that nature is so constituted as to involve many cause—effect sequences. A flooded basement usually follows a rain; the movement of a ball across a level surface implies an earlier event, which set the ball in motion; a distant clap of thunder implies a prior electrical phenomenon. A cause—effect sequence prescribes the order of events, and memories of those events will usually be ordered correctly. Yet, to infer order from presumed cause—effect sequences may not be without error. An automobile lying in a ditch, an auto on which a tire is obviously blown, may lead to the conclusion that the blowout antedated the accident and was the cause for loss of control of the auto. In fact the blowout may have occurred after the loss of control of the car.

Laboratory studies do not normally deal directly with such cause—effect event sequences. Perhaps the closest counterpart is that represented by serial learning. A serial task, of course, is one in which the events must be ordered in a specified manner. It is certainly not my intent to review the vast amount of work on serial learning; this has been done admirably by Harcum (1975). The difficulties of determining the processes involved in serial learning make such learning somewhat of a mystery, and even the very recent work seems only to deepen the mystery (e.g., Saufley, 1975). Serial associations, of whatever they are constituted, contain information from which the order of events may be correctly inferred. We have all learned the alphabet as a serial task. *A* does not really cause *B*, and *B* does not really cause *C*, but that *B* comes before *C*, and *A* before *B*, gives these relationships almost a functional cause— effect status. Furthermore, because these associations are usually asymmetrical (*Q* will elicit *R* much more readily than *R* will elicit *Q*), they provide relatively direct information about order. Many investigators have asked subjects to identify the positions held by items in a serial task after a certain amount of learning had occurred. The data to be reported as Experiment 4 used a similar approach. This study was described briefly in an earlier publication (Underwood, 1969a).

EXPERIMENT 4

The subjects were presented 25 words, each for 5 seconds, after which they were asked to identify the position held by each word in the list. The words were given aurally by tape, and the subjects were fully instructed about the nature of the test before the list was presented. They were further told that there were 25 words in the list. After the list was presented, test sheets were distributed and explained. The 25 words were listed in random order, and the subject was requested to assign a number to each to represent its position in the list. To prevent the use of a number more than once, a list of the numbers from 1 to 25 was provided on the test sheet and the subjects checked off each number as it was used. The 25 words were of relatively low frequency. Records were available for 100 college student subjects.

The number of hits, defined as assigning the correct position to a word, is shown in Figure 5. Since 100 subjects were tested, the values on the ordinate may be translated directly into percentages. Thus, 97% of the subjects correctly identified the position of the first word in the list. Primacy and recency effects are very much in evidence. Given a closed system for identifying positions and

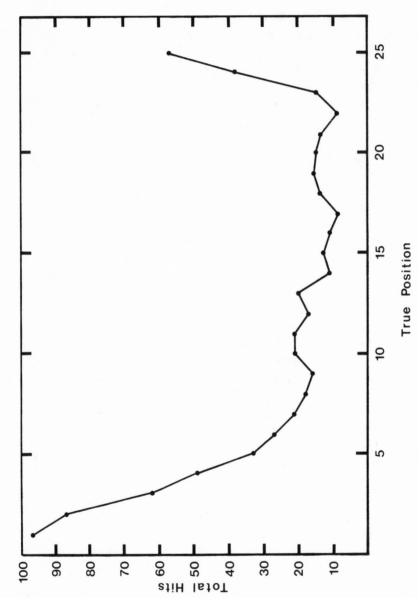

FIGURE 5. Number of hits (identifying the correct position of a word) for each of 25 words presented once for study (Experiment 4).

24

given that the subjects were most frequently correct on primacy and recency items, it must follow that, in general, the positions of the items in the first half of the list were likely to be assigned positions that overestimated the true positions, and items in the second half were likely to be assigned positions that underestimated true positions. It also follows that variability in judgments should be less for items in the middle of the list than for those holding positions on both sides of the middle (e.g., positions 5–10 and 15–20). Although not evident in Figure 5, both of these phenomena were quite evident in the data.

Was serial learning involved? The subjects were interrogated about the "strategies" they used. Two answers predominated. First, a verbal label was used for the first item, and a "last" label was used by some subjects for the last item, this being assigned when the list terminated. Some subjects indicated that more general labels were used for several items, such phrases as the "first part of list" and "last part of list." The other common report was that items were associated in succession, this being accomplished by rehearsal and by mediators. One remarkable subject correctly identified the position of all 25 words; she indicated that she had simply associated the words in a chain, and when I requested it, she did in fact produce most of the list. Some of the subjects actually wrote the first several items on the test sheet before assigning numbers.

Such evidence is by no means conclusive concerning the role of serial learning in the judgments, but it is strongly suggestive. The evidence also indicates that subjects may construct calendarlike devices, in which they try to associate the words in particular portions of the lists with appropriate labels. I think we must accept the fact that serial learning, whatever the processes that underlie it, may serve as a means of inferring temporal information. The data from Experiment 2 showed that correct decisions concerning ordering were slightly better when the lag between two words was zero than when the lag was one. I believe this can be taken as evidence that serial associations between the two words were developed and that decisions of recency were made on this basis.

EXPOSURE DURATION

As a general principle, it can be said that the longer the exposure period or study time allotted an item, the better or greater the learning. There are cases in which the improvement is minimal as time increases beyond a given value, but it would be quite unexpected if performance became poorer with increased time. Insofar as temporal coding is based upon attributes that are acquired during the exposure period of an item, we would expect temporal coding to be directly facilitated by exposure duration. When a notorious public event occurs, no matter how brief the event per se may be, the possibility of establishing a temporal code may extend over several days as the event is rehashed, its implications examined, and its relationships with other events noted. We have no idea concerning the true exposure duration for the events used in Experiment 1. To examine the influence of such a variable we must turn to the control offered by the laboratory. However, this variable produces difficult problems within the laboratory, and we must examine these problems before getting to the substance of the influence of exposure duration.

Problems of Method

Thus far, only two general techniques for testing temporal ordering of memories have been discussed: the within-task and the between-task techniques. The test for within-task studies may be a request for the subject to order all items, as in Experiment 4, or to make recency and lag judgments on selected pairs, as in Experiment 2. There are several other variants with which we must become acquainted in order to pursue the discussion.

A variant on the within-task method might be called the continuous within-list procedure as opposed to the use of discrete lists. In the continuous technique, the subject is given a long series of words. Periodically, a test is given, perhaps requiring a few seconds. Then further words are presented for study, another test administered, more study, and so on. On any given test the subject might be presented two target words, T1 and T2, and is asked to make a recency judgment, and perhaps a lag judgment in addition. Several published studies (e.g., Peterson, Johnson & Coatney, 1969) have used the same item in recency judgments. The word is presented twice, and, on its second occurrence, the subject is asked to give a lag judgment (number of other words that occurred between the first presentation of the target and its present occurrence). Obviously, the question the subject must answer is how recent was the first presentation of the target word.

In a still further variation, the subject may be presented a closed system of units, and these units are used over and over. Thus, Hinrichs (1970) used only 18 different letters in the many tests given his subjects. This was carried to a further extreme by Hinrichs and Buschke (1970). They presented only eight different letters. After an initial presentation of the letters, the testing began in a continuous-list procedure. As each letter was presented, the subject made a judgment as to which of the other seven letters was the "oldest" letter; that is, which letter of the seven had the longest lag since last presentation. This procedure produced extremely orderly data, with the choice of the correct letter increasing directly and linearly as age of the correct letter increased.

Finally, by way of a brief survey of techniques, it should be noted that in the continuous procedure it is possible to vary the T2–test interval. That is, not only may the lag be varied (T1–T2 interval), but the length of the retention interval—the T2–test interval—may also be varied. We may now return to the problem of method involved in studying exposure duration.

Consider the discrete within-list procedure. Suppose that for one group of subjects the exposure duration of each item in the list was two seconds, and for the same list with another group the duration was four seconds. After each list is presented, tests are given, these tests being the same for both lists. Suppose further that we calculate various measures of the accuracy of temporal encoding and find that the performances on the two lists do not differ. The apparent conclusion is that exposure duration is of no consequence for these judgments. However, it can be seen that because duration of exposure differed, the retention interval differed for the two lists, the differences being the greatest for items occurring in the initial positions in the two lists. We could keep the retention interval constant by testing for all items in the lists presented at a two-second rate and for only the last half of the items presented at a four-second rate, but insofar as memory is influenced by the position of the items in the list, a confounding would still be present.

We will next consider the continuous within-list procedure, again with two exposure durations as the independent variable. The series may be illustrated with A representing the target word, and x representing the intervening words:

$$A\ x\ x\ x\ x\ x\ x\ x\ x\ x\ x\ x\ x\ A?$$

In this case, the temporal interval between the first and second occurrence of A will differ as a function of exposure duration of the items. Although the interval per se might seem to be inconsequential as compared with the number of intervening items (which are equal in number for the two exposure durations), this would prejudge the influence of an independent variable. Indeed, so far as I have been able to determine, there has been no systematic manipulation of the number of intervening words, keeping the interval constant, nor has the reverse been done.

I bring up these pesky problems because, in the few studies I have found that have manipulated exposure duration, there seems to be no consensus concerning its influence (Guenther & Linton, 1975; Peterson, 1967; Lassen, Daniel & Bartlett, 1974; Berlyne, 1966). Only Berlyne attempted to adjust for the intrinsic confounding in the studies, and he concluded that the ordering of a set of objects, seen once, was uninfluenced by exposure duration.

One solution to the problem seems to be through the use of exposure duration as a within-list variable. It could be carried out by either the continuous or discrete-list procedures. The critical need is to vary the exposure duration of T1 and T2 without a concomitant variation in the T1—T2 interval or in the number of items falling between T1 and T2. Thus, the duration of exposure for all items within the lag interval would be constant across the conditions in which the T1 and T2 exposure duration is varied. We could have several critical target pairs within the list, or different lags within the list, but across lists we could balance out positions within the lists and still have several lags. Such an experiment has not been done.

There is another solution. Remember that we are trying to determine the role of the independent variable—duration of exposure—on the acquisition of temporal information. We need not necessarily make our tests by using pairs of words. We can request temporal information (position information) for all items in the list and simply vary the temporal duration of items during study, using a sufficient number of lists or a sufficiently long list so that items given varying durations of exposure will be equally represented at various positions in the list(s). I will shortly report such an experiment, but one more problem must be evaluated before we can be confident of the method.

Instructional Variables

In a study which Joel Zimmerman and I did a few years ago (Zimmerman & Underwood, 1968), the nature of the instructions was manipulated. The subject was given 12 successive lists for free recall, the lists containing either 8 or 12 words. Each list was recalled immediately after presentation, and then a final free recall of all items in all lists was requested. Next, the subjects were given the 12 lists, each printed on an index card, and were requested to order the lists to correspond to the order of learning. Finally, a pair of words from each list was shown the subjects, and they were requested to identify which of the two occurred earliest in the list. There were three groups of subjects differing only in the instructions they received prior to learning the 12 lists. One group was given only the usual free-recall instructions. A second group received the free-recall instructions plus information that they would be tested for the order of the *lists*, and the third group received the instructions of the second group plus the information that they would also be tested for order of the words *within* the lists.

The results showed that the groups did not differ in free-recall performance, nor did they differ on position knowledge, although the position knowledge they acquired was substantial. For example, on the within-list tests for the order of the two words within the lists, the average subject correctly ordered 10 of the 12 pairs. We were led to conclude that "relating the spatial–temporal dimension to events to be memorized is a fundamental characteristic of the learning process" (p. 307). Others, as I do now, may feel a little uneasy about this conclusion as a generalized statement. There are two reasons. First, the method of study was complete presentation; the subject was given each list on a card and was allowed 40 seconds to study the words. This contrasts with most other studies where each word was presented singly for study. Second (and this may follow from the first), free recall as a function of position showed no recency effect, although recall was given immediately upon the termination of the study period. There was a very clear primacy effect extending through the first five positions in the list. I now believe that it is possible that the learning of each list was primarily by serial association and that these associations were probably responsible for the within-list recency judgments. This mechanism would not, of course, account for the equal knowledge of list position shown by the subjects in the three groups.

The question at issue is whether or not subjects can influence their temporal judgments when the nature of the temporal test is explained to them. Will they code or rehearse differently for such a test from the way in which they might for a free-recall test? The issue is of some importance in considering exposure duration as an independent variable in the mixed-list case, a procedure which seems on other grounds to be quite appropriate. Will the rehearsal pattern of subjects differ when they are given a long exposure to an item, as compared to a short exposure, but when they are not expecting a temporal test? Expecting only free recall, the subjects might displace rehearsal far back into the list and, thereby, distort position information. The likelihood of this happening may be directly related to exposure duration.

The evidence available indicates that this is not a serious problem. Proctor and Ambler (1975) gave subjects a long list of words for study, telling the subjects only that a memory test would be given. The subjects in one group were strongly urged to rehearse previous items, in addition to the items present at the moment. The subjects in a second group were urged to restrict their attention only to the word present at the moment. Proctor and Ambler found that, on lag judgments for repeated words, performance was uninfluenced by the instructions. On lag judgments for two different words, there was an effect that was inconsistent (depending on lag), but the subjects who were requested to displace rehearsals did more poorly than the other group only on judgments involving long lags. Tzeng (1976), in perhaps still stronger tests, reached the conclusion that displaced rehearsals did not influence temporal judgments and believes that the attributes entering into temporal judgments are established on the first occurrence of a word and that subsequent rehearsals of that word are quite irrelevant.

The gross outcome of the data to be reported as Experiment 5 was described in another publication (Underwood, 1969a). Those data indicated that exposure duration had little influence on position judgments. Several different groups were given the lists used in Experiment 5, and for some of these groups the interest was in free recall as a function of the massing and distribution of repeated items. These recall data were presented as Experiments I and II in an earlier publication (Underwood, 1969b), and they showed that recall was better for items that were distributed than for those that were massed, but that recall for the massed items did increase as number of occurrences of a word increased. The rate of increase was simply greater for items that were given by distributed schedules.

Experiment 5

Each subject studied a list containing 52 words, but because 24 of the words occurred two or more times, there were actually 100 positions in the lists. Twenty-eight words occurred once, 8 occurred twice, 8 three times, and 8 four times. Items that occurred multiply were further divided into massed items and distributed items. When an item was massed, it occupied adjacent positions in the series; when it was distributed, at least one other item fell between occurrences. The list was presented orally and a single presentation of an item involved a 5-second period during which the word was spoken twice. Thus, words were presented 1, 2, 3, or 4 times, or for 5, 10, 15, and 20 seconds. Items were rotated across three forms to avoid the likelihood that item function and item difficulty would be confounded. In presenting the results, the data for all forms have been combined. Each form was given to 22 subjects, hence data on a total of 66 subjects were available.

The subjects were instructed as is normally done for free-recall learning, and these instructions included the statement that order of the items was quite unimportant for the memory test to be given. (Appropriate apologies and explanations were given after the experiment for this misleading aspect of the instructions.) After the list was presented, the subjects were given booklets in which the 52 words were listed in random order along the left side of the sheets. They were informed that they were to make estimates of the position held by each word in the list. For words having multiple occurrences, the subjects were told to estimate the position of *last* occurrence of the word. In making their judgments of position, the subjects drew horizontal lines opposite each word, a long line indicating that the word was in an early position in the list, a short line indicating that it was near the end of the list. The subjects were warned to look over several words before starting to produce the lines, so that no problem would arise by a need to draw a line that was longer than the paper was wide. The lines drawn were measured to the nearest 1/10 inch. Position within the list and line length were inversely related. However, in presenting correlational evidence, the values will be reported as positive.

Estimated position and true position.   Across the three forms, there were 84 words that had been presented once. For each of these words, a mean line length was determined by averaging across the line lengths produced by the 22 subjects given the word for study. A plot of these 84 means against true position showed a very evident relationship. The product—moment correlation was .75. Because of a primacy effect, there was some deviation from linearity in the plot. When a nonlinear measure (*eta*) of the relationship was calculated, the value was .82.

Hintzman and Block (1971) presented their subjects 50 three-letter nouns under instructions to remember the words for a later memory test. Each word was presented for five seconds on the study trial. On the test, the subjects were asked to estimate the tenth of the list occupied by each word on the study trial. Their plot between the true position and estimated position showed a very clear relationship. Flexser and Bower (1974) used lists of 34 words and followed much the same procedure as that used by Hintzman and Block. Again a relationship was found relating true position and estimated position.

This brings us to a seeming contradiction, which will cling to us throughout several chapters. Suppose we have presented lists for study, as was done in the above experiments. On the tests, however, rather than asking for position judgments for each word separately, we present the subject pairs of words from the list and ask for lag judgments: How many other words fell between these two words? Since single words were positioned with some accuracy, it would seem that lag judgments for the pairs would appropriately reflect lag differences. This seems not to be the case. In at least two studies (Hintzman & Block, 1973; Hintzman, Summers, & Block, 1975), there was no relationship between true lag and the lag estimates. How can a subject make a reasonably valid position judgment for a single item from a list and be quite incapable of making a valid lag judgment for two words from the list? It will be remembered that we did find some relationship between true lag and lag judgments for pairs of words in Experiment 2, Chapter 1. However, by way of anticipation, an experiment in which we found no relationship between lag and lag judgments for pairs of words will be reported in Chapter 4. Furthermore, we found that subjects literally could not learn to improve their judgments over trials. This is why I say the problem is not one we can avoid as we proceed through additional experiments.

To return to the central variable, it will be remembered that we are asking about the role of duration of exposure on temporal coding. Because of the way in which the lists for Experiment 5 were constructed, the range of positions differed for the items presented once and for the last occurrence of those presented under the massed schedule. It differed still more for the items presented once and for the last occurrence of those presented under the distributed schedule. To adjust for this, the following steps were taken. First, the words presented 2, 3, and 4 times were considered as a group. Each subject had 12 such words, 4 at each frequency level. It was possible to select 12 words that had been presented once and that also held positions that matched closely, item for item, the last occurrence of those 12 words that had been presented 2, 3, and 4 times. It was therefore feasible to compare position judgments for the words presented once and those presented more than once, with the average duration of the latter being 15 seconds versus 5 seconds for the items presented once.

For each subject, a product–moment correlation was calculated between true position and line length for the 12 items presented once, and a separate correlation was done for the 12 massed items presented for an average of 15 seconds. Each correlation was transformed into a z' score, and the significance of the mean difference of the two distributions of 66 z' values was determined. The mean z' for the words presented once was .46 ($r = .43$), and for those occurring 2, 3, and 4, times, the mean z' was .57 ($r = .52$). These two means did not differ reliably ($t = 1.81$).

We may now examine the results for the 12 words presented under the distributed schedule. The results for these words do not, of course, tell us about temporal coding as a function of exposure duration. Nevertheless, the results are of interest in asking whether a subject can distinguish between the position of last occurrence of an item and the positions of earlier occurrences.

For the 12 words presented under distributed schedules, the range of positions of last occurrence was more restricted than for the words presented under the massed schedule. Nevertheless, it was possible to obtain 12 words presented once that, item for item, essentially had equivalent positions to the last occurrence of the items given the distributed schedule. Again, product–moment correlations were determined for each subject for each of the two types of items, and the z' transformation was applied. The mean z' for the words presented once was .17 ($r = .17$), and for the distributed words, .28 ($r = .28$). These two means did not differ ($t = 1.84$). Even with the restricted range of positions involved, the mean z' for the 12 words presented once differed reliably from zero ($t = 3.77$). For the words given the massed schedules, the above data indicate that position knowledge was not appreciably better for words with multiple occurrences than for words given once. The temporal duration or exposure of a word during study seems to have little effect on the knowledge of position that may develop during study. The fact that the words given multiple occurrences were somewhat more accurately positioned than those given once, although not reliably so, may reflect the fact that some of the words presented once simply may not have been recognized (on the test) as having been in the list.

The data were examined in still another way, to evaluate the effect of exposure duration. A mean position judgment was determined for each word by summing across subjects. Thus, for words given massed presentation, a total of 36 different words was used across the three forms. Mean position estimates and true positions were correlated. For the massed items, the value was .83, and for the 36 distributed items, .52. For the 36 words given a single presentation but matched on position with the massed words, the correlation was .79. The corresponding value for the words presented once and matched on position with words under the distributed schedule was .51. These outcomes merely support the earlier conclusion that duration of exposure seems to be of little consequence for position judgments.

Positioning and recall.   In a second study using these lists, the subjects were instructed to attend only to the word being presented at the moment. There were 60 subjects, 20 for each form. This instruction had no effect on overall recall. After the subjects had recalled, they were given the list of 52 words and were requested to make direct position judgments. In this task, they were to assign a number between 1 and 100 to indicate the position of last occurrence of the word. As a measure of positioning accuracy, the deviation of each word from true position was calculated for each of the 52 words for each subject. The mean deviation for each word was then calculated.

The pattern of correlations between true and estimated position was found to be much the same as in the first study, although all of the correlations were a little lower. While it is possible that the act of recalling may have disturbed knowledge of position, the results taken at face value confirm the work of other investigators, in that instructions to attend only to the item present at the moment (and not to displace rehearsal) did not give evidence of increased knowledge of position. Of greater interest is the relationship between position knowledge and recall.

A mean deviation score was determined for each subject, using all 52 words in the list, and these values were correlated with total recall for the 60 subjects. The product–moment correlation was −.04. The positioning error for massed items that were recalled and for those that were not was determined for each subject. The mean positioning error for recalled items was 25.53, for those not recalled, 27.19. The difference was not reliable ($t = .80$). The same outcome was found for the words given distributed schedules. The only evidence found that related recall and position estimates involved the words presented once. The words recalled from among the 28 possible gave a mean positioning error that was less than those not recalled, and the difference was reliable ($t = 4.11$). Such evidence is hard to interpret because the items not recalled may also not have been recognized when the position-judgment test was given. Goodwin and Bruce (1972) have concluded that temporal tags are relatively unimportant as recall cues for the words in the initial portion of a free-recall task. In general, the evidence from the present experiment would extend this to all positions in a free-recall task, although this may not hold in the recency area of the list when recall is given immediately after presentation.

The data that have been evaluated in this section indicate that position learning or temporal coding does not seem to be related critically to the duration of an item during study. In a strict sense, this cannot be true. An item must be exposed for some minimal amount of time for a temporal code to be established. The evidence indicates that beyond this unknown minimal amount of time, further exposure does not add appreciably to the temporal code.

INTERFERENCE IN TEMPORAL CODING

If we study serial learning as a function of the similarity of items within the list, whether formal or meaningful similarity, we know that the learning is impeded as similarity increases. It might seem inevitable, therefore, that recency judgments or lag judgments would be influenced by similarity. This inevitability is by no means assured. First, we do not know the basic attributes involved in serial learning, and second, we have not yet identified, with any sureness, the nature of the attributes involved in temporal coding. We will examine three elementary situations that might be used in studying the influence of interference in temporal coding:

$A\, x\, x\, x\, x\, x\, x\, x\, x\, x\, x\, A$ (identical word)
$A\, x\, x\, x\, x\, x\, x\, x\, x\, x\, x\, A'$ (associated words)
$A\, x\, x\, x\, x\, x\, x\, x\, x\, x\, x\, B$ (unrelated words)

Assume that these series are presented within a long list, and then, after the list is completed, the subject is requested to make position judgments. In the case of repeated words, we have seen that even if a word occurs as many as four times within a list, separated by other words on each occurrence, the position identification for *last* occurrence is as accurate as for the single occurrence of a word. Although we do not know how accurate performance would have been for the first occurrence of a repeated word, the evidence suggests that each occurrence is attended by some type of positional encoding that distinguishes it from its earlier positional encodings. What would we anticipate in the case of associated words? When A occurs, a strong associate to it may occur implicitly. Thus, when *table* represents A, the implicit response *chair* may occur, and perhaps also the implicit response may be given temporal coding along with the word actually presented (*table*). Later in the series A' occurs, which in this instance might be *chair*. It is not unreasonable to expect *table* to occur implicitly to *chair*, and perhaps be temporally coded at that point. If all of these events do in fact occur, each of the two words will carry temporal codes about two locations. Where will the subject estimate the position of each word to be?

There is some similarity between this case and the one in which the same word occurs two or more times, although there are differences. When the same word occurs twice, there are two different temporal codes for the same word. In the case of associated words, the two different words may both be associated with two different temporal codes, these codes being identical. The two cases are much like the differences between the $A-B$, $A-D$ and the $A-B$, $A-Br$ paradigms in a retroactive inhibition test.

Among the published experiments, one by Hintzman, Summers, and Block (1975) used the above cases (which include the two unrelated words). Subjects were asked for lag judgments, and this was the experiment in which the lag judgments for unrelated words showed no relationship to true lag. Since the associated words did produce a relationship between true lag and lag judgments, it might be concluded that there is no support for the expectations of confusion. Yet, the associated words did differ from the unrelated words, so that the associates were in some way playing a role. In fact, the lag judgments for the associated words more closely approximated the true lags when these lags were long than did the lag judgments for repeated words.

Earlier it was pointed out that recency judgments and lag judgments can be conceptually independent. This independence seemed to be contradicted in Experiment 2, where only unrelated words were used. It remains possible that with associated words the two could be independent. We will present an experiment in a later chapter that shows that the number of correct recency judgments is quite unrelated to the separation between the two words tested, so the issue is by no means closed. It is perhaps possible that had Hintzman et al. (1975) requested position judgments or presented the associates as a pair and asked for the identification of the most recent word, performance would have been quite different from that obtained by lag judgments. Of course, there is no implication in the above that the response measure used by Hintzman and his colleagues is inappropriate; their interest was in quite a different matter than the one of interest in this section.

To determine directly the role of interference in temporal coding, a simple test would involve two conditions:

$A \, x \, x \, x \, x \, x \, A' \, x \, x \, x \, x \, x$ Test: A versus A'
$A \, x \, x \, x \, x \, x \, B \, x \, x \, x \, x \, x$ Test: A versus B

A and A' represent associated words, and A and B, unrelated words. The test would consist of recency judgments. Perhaps the test is not quite as simple as it seems. Because two associated words are likely to be more readily recognized as having been in the list, as compared with two unrelated words, it would be necessary to remove this factor as a source of contamination. To test only pairs for which both words are recognized produces both a subject and item selection with unknown influences. Perhaps the most likely approach would be to use short lists in which pilot work shows that essentially all subjects will recognize all items.

At the present time, the possible sources of interference in within-list temporal codes simply have not received the attention necessary to reach conclusions. Although I undertook an experiment along the lines suggested by the above paradigm, I did not adequately solve the problem of differential recognition, and time pressures have not allowed a followup, although one of the experiments to be reported later is related to the problem. We will see later that considerable information is available dealing with between-list interference on the establishment and perseverance of temporal codes.

STRENGTH

Memories may be said to differ in strength. Under most circumstances, multiple occurrences of a given event will result in a stronger memory than will a single occurrence. The differences in strength are most easily inferred from differences in recall. It is reasonable to ask, therefore, whether this property of memories (strength) may enter into judgments of temporal order, hence may be said to be involved in temporal coding.

Let us say that T1 and T2 are presented at different points in time as parts of a task to be learned. Subsequently, they are presented to the subjects and a recency judgment requested. What is required for subjects to utilize strength as a property that would yield a correct recency decision? First, the subjects must be able to assess differences in strength (a strength scanner?), and, second, they must apply the rule relating decreasing strength (forgetting) to the passage of time. In so doing, they must reach the decision that the weakest of the two memories is the oldest. This may be stated in another way. Assume that the strength of the two target memories, T1 and T2, were equivalent at the time of formation, and both weaken at equivalent rates over time. This can only mean that, at the time of the recency judgment, T2 is stronger than T1, and, if this property is used to distinguish age, T2 will be judged to be the most recent memory.

As is true with so many theories, the strength hypothesis runs into trouble with data. Two such instances may be noted in the data presented earlier. In Experiment 2, the subjects did not conclude that two events, whose order they could not determine, must have been presented close together in time. Implementation of the correlation (two events that are indistinguishable in order must have occurred close together in time) would have been expected on strict empirical grounds, and it would also have been expected if the subjects were reaching their decisions on the basis of strength of the memories. In Experiment 4, had subjects been asked to recall, it would be expected that the initial items presented in the list would have shown the best recall—would have been of highest strength. A strength hypothesis, with no other factors involved, would predict that these words would have been positioned after the words that occurred in the middle of the list. In Experiment 5, words presented only five seconds for study were positioned with about equal accuracy as words presented for longer study periods, and these latter words were better recalled than the former. Age judgments were not correlated with strength.

The strength hypothesis is an appealing one, and has been worked out with considerable precision (e.g., Hinrichs, 1970). Yet, it is obviously wrong when viewed as a single-factor theory. Experiments that have been devised explicitly to test a strength hypothesis have frequently used at least the following two paradigms:

T1 T1 $x\,x\,x\,x\,x$ T2 $x\,x\,x\,x\,x$ Test
T1 $x\,x\,x\,x\,x$ T2 $x\,x\,x\,x\,x$ Test

The test consists in both cases of a comparative recency judgment between T1 and T2. The idea is that there will be more errors in the paradigm where T1 has occurred twice than in the paradigm where it has occurred once; that is, this would be true if strength alone determines the decisions. Now, in fact, there is some disagreement as to the outcome of such tests (some illustrative studies: Flexner & Bower, 1974; Galbraith, 1975a; Galbraith, 1976; Peterson, Johnson

& Coatney, 1969). There is no intent to try to resolve these differences here. We can be reasonably sure that strength cannot be accepted as a single principle for assessing the temporal order of events. Yet, we would not reject strength completely as a possible contributor to a complex of attributes that may be involved in temporal coding.

In any extreme form, a strength theory faces a difficult logical problem. An extreme strength theory would say that when the same event occurs two or more times, a single trace of the event is established; each successive occurrence of the event simply makes the single trace stronger. If this is taken literally, a problem arises: If we present the same item twice, separated by other items, and, upon the second presentation ask the subjects for a lag judgment, they simply could not comply. They could not comply because there would not be two events in their memory, only a strong single event. But the facts are that subjects can readily comply with such a request and their lag judgments are (in some situations) related to true lag (see Wells, 1974, for a more detailed discussion of this and related issues). Any assumption that strength is used to infer the age of memories must also assume that other information (no matter how crude) is carried in memory, which will allow a distinction between the two occurrences of the same nominal event. When this approach is pursued to its logical end, the other extreme form of theorizing is reached, namely, that each occurrence of an event establishes a unique trace (the multitrace hypothesis). Of course, at this extreme, the theorizing must incorporate some mechanism or process by which the separate traces may in some way unite, combine, or sum if we are to accept the fairly obvious fact that frequency of occurrence and strength (as inferred from recall) are directly related.

As a single factor, strength cannot possibly mediate temporal judgments. But there is no evidence that functional strength, however constituted, is completely irrelevant to all judgments concerning the ordering of memories on the time dimension. We know that subjects can make reasonably accurate decisions concerning the relative frequency with which words occur in printed discourse. Carroll and White (1973) asked subjects to make judgments of the point in their lives (from age 2 years) at which they first learned each of 220 nouns. These judgments correlated quite highly with word frequency. Thus, in a sense, the strongest (most frequent) words were the oldest. Of course, there are other ways to view such data, but the point of the moment is that we should not preempt strength as a possible factor among other factors involved in the temporal ordering of memories.

EVENT FREQUENCY

In experiments similar to Experiment 2, the subject is given two words from the list just presented and asked to estimate the number of other words that occurred between T1 and T2. Could it be that subjects have kept a running count of the number of different words (events) and use this information to make their estimates? Such a possibility has been suggested (e.g., Berlyne, 1966; Lockhart, 1969). It is known that, if words are repeated with varying frequencies in a list, the subjects assimilate with some accuracy these relative frequencies. Thus, if the subjects can "count" different events (different words) in much the same way as they can count the frequencies of repeated events (same words), it appears that temporal judgments might in part be mediated by frequency information. There are problems with this idea. The subjects don't know which words are going to serve the T1 and T2 functions on the test. Effectively, then, at the time of test, they have to use other information to identify the locus of the words in the study list before, say, making a lag judgment based on the number of words that have intervened. The critical question concerns the way in which the positions of the words are identified in the first place.

To conclude that in the common case it is difficult to see how event frequency can mediate temporal ordering is not to imply that frequency of events is irrelevant to judgments of temporal ordering. In the usual experiment, the time between two targets is perfectly confounded with the number of events. It is not unreasonable to ask whether the recency judgment for T1 and T2 would be influenced if this correlation was broken. For example, the number of different events between two targets could be manipulated. One way would be to vary the rate of presentation of the events occurring between the two target events (e.g., 5 items at a two-second rate versus 10 items at a one-second rate). Another way would be to vary the number of different events that intervene, holding the rate constant. In the extreme case, we would have a blank interval between the two target events. I have not found such experiments reported in the literature. For the time being, therefore, it must be concluded that the influence of event frequency between T1 and T2 on recency and lag judgments is unknown.

CONTEXT

No single concept is so widely used in theories of memory functioning as is the concept of context. Context, when we attempt to give it operational meaning, refers to characteristics of the external environment, characteristics of tasks in which the subject may be engaged, and characteristics of the mental environment resulting directly or indirectly from the experimental procedures imposed. Although context is widely used theoretically, it is probably correct to say that never in the history of choice of theoretical mechanisms has one been chosen that has so little support in direct evidence. Although studies, which seem to implicate true context effects, can be found in the literature (e.g., Falkenburg, 1972; Godden & Baddeley, 1975), there are many other published studies that fail to show reliable effects, and, because of a tendency for editors not to publish negative results, one can only guess that there are scores of unpublished studies that show no effects of context manipulations. Of course, it is perfectly reasonable to use context as a purely abstract theoretical term, but most theorists do not use the term in this manner.

Why has there been so much theorizing using a mechanism that is on shaky grounds empirically? There seems to be two reasons. First, in many areas, some such concept seems absolutely necessary: A theory might not be able to get off the ground without it or might be found incomplete at some stage without it. Second, there is at least anecdotal evidence in support of the fact that a particular memory may be associated with a particular context. Nearly every member of my generation can tell exactly where he or she was and what he or she was doing when given the information that the Japanese had attacked Pearl Harbor. Such illustrations can be multiplied by any observer. In understanding the spoken language, we know that the meaning to be inferred from certain words depends upon the momentary context established by the meaning of other words.

It will come as no surprise to realize that we often attempt to relate temporal encoding to context. In doing this, however, the theory must face problems that are not faced when applied to other memory phenomena. We might recall a certain event because of its association (occurred in conjunction with) another more memorable event. No temporal coding is implied by this phenomenon. But, if the temporal ordering of two events is mediated by differential contexts for T1 and T2 (because the contexts are more memorable than T1 and T2), there must be some basis for asserting also that the two sets of contextual memories may be ordered more readily than the target memories.

If the two different contexts (associated with T1 and T2) have an intrinsic order such that it corresponds to a cause-effect sequence or to another type of time metric (e.g., calendar dates), there can be no doubt that context could lead to correct temporal ordering of T1 and T2, an ordering that would not have been possible without the contexts. Such an effect has been demonstrated (Guenther & Linton, 1975), and it makes clear that context can mediate proper ordering of target memories. But, how can contexts, without a built-in temporal ordering, mediate ordering? How can context differences lead to better temporal ordering than T1 and T2? If we assume that T1 was in a red context, T2 in a blue context, and that the associations between targets and contexts were established, the question concerns how it is possible for red and blue to be better ordered than T1 and T2. That contexts without a built-in ordering system can influence the temporal coding of associated target memories does not seem possible. Nevertheless, in keeping with the tentative atmosphere that I have tried to establish in this chapter, the matter will not be closed. Several experiments in which context was manipulated will be reported in Chapter 5.

SUMMARY

In this chapter, I have given some information about the facts and theories that were available to us. This was not viewed as a comprehensive survey of the literature. For example, I have not covered certain experiments dealing with characteristics of the events, such as words versus pictures (e.g., Fozard, 1970), words versus nonsense syllables (e.g., Flexser & Bower, 1974), or low versus high association value of syllables (Wolff, 1966). Such studies have not been dismissed as being irrelevant to my inquiry; rather, I found such studies produced intrinsic difficulties of interpretation, which I chose not to pursue in this book.

As noted in the first chapter, the interest in temporal coding was instigated by some puzzling results on temporal differentiation between lists in which the proactive inhibition paradigm was involved. In attempting to acquire some understanding of the mechanisms involved in producing the puzzle, I was led to a number of experiments involving both within-list and between-list manipulations. In effect, I carried out two lines of research. In this process, my interest began to expand to include problems of temporal coding in general. In presenting the experiments in the next chapters, I found it most compatible to proceed historically. For some of the experiments, this was quite necessary, and so it was adopted as a general plan.

3
The Puzzle

I have long held a deep affection for the phenomenon of proactive inhibition. It has not always returned this affection. At times it has behaved in quite unexpected ways and has seemed particularly reluctant to accept my theoretical gifts. In view of these experiences with proactive inhibition, I suppose that I should have been prepared for the series of events that I will relate in this and the following chapter. I was not prepared for them, and I am convinced they would never have happened except for one of those casual or incidental decisions that are inevitably necessary in designing experiments. This decision will become exposed in due time. It is necessary first to give the background for a major experiment we undertook in the fall of 1971.

THE BACKGROUND

Proactive inhibition is a retention loss for a particular task attributed to the prior learning of other tasks. More strictly speaking, the loss is measured against a control group that is not given prior learning. Proactive inhibition and its earlier discovered kin, retroactive inhibition, have been thought to be the basic paradigms for all forgetting both within and outside the laboratory. They are linked together through the common general interpretative concept of interference, a concept brought to the fore in 1932 as a result of McGeoch's methical and logical destruction of alternatives, and by his masterful summing up of the evidence for interference-like effects in retroactive inhibition. Given this orientation, the development of our experimental knowledge for both retroactive and proactive inhibition hinged on the selection of independent variables that would cause the amount of interference to vary. With theoretical elaboration (Underwood & Postman, 1960), it seemed that a rather comprehensive theory of forgetting was available. Alas, this was not to be. The theory could not be supported in the manner it demanded. This failure was not interpreted to mean that proactive and retroactive inhibition were not basic to the understanding of forgetting; rather, it was taken to mean that something had been overlooked in working out the details of the interference mechanisms.

In casting about for insights that might be used to revise the theory, Bruce Ekstrand and I undertook an experiment on proactive inhibition in which one of the independent variables was the distribution of learning of the interfering list (Underwood & Ekstrand, 1966). We used the A-B, A-D interference paradigm for paired-associate lists, hence the distribution of practice was applied to the learning of $A-B$. Among other conditions, the subject was given 32 trials on $A-B$. Under the distributed conditions, eight trials were given on four successive days (Monday, Tuesday, Wednesday, and Thursday). Immediately after the $A-B$ trials on Thursday, $A-D$ learning was administered until the subject attained a criterion of one perfect trial. On Friday, 24 hours after learning $A-D$, it was recalled. Although we did not have a control condition (only $A-D$ learning) we knew that the recall scores we observed were so high that essentially there was no proactive inhibition, and this presumption was fully supported in later studies. In another condition, all 32 trials on $A-B$ were given just prior to the learning of $A-D$ on Thursday. This massing of the $A-B$ trials resulted in very heavy proactive interference in the 24-hour recall scores for $A-D$.

In interpreting the above finding, it seemed possible that the distribution of $A-B$ trials over days resulted in the establishment of a clear differentiation between the two lists, a differentiation that allowed the subject to identify the response terms perfectly with each list so that the interference was minimal. Differentiation was simply another way of speaking of a temporal discrimination. In another experiment, Keppel (1964) had shown that if the learning of the A-D list was distributed over days (with $A-B$ massed), the forgetting of A-D was markedly diminished. It appeared, therefore, that the distributed learning (over days) of either the $A-B$ or $A-D$ tasks markedly diminished proactive interference. This was not only a conclusion of great practical importance, but also seemed to indicate that the temporal differentiation between interfering tasks was

extremely critical in determining the amount of proactive interference.

It can be seen, however, that the critical independent variable
could not be identified with confidence in the Underwood—Ekstrand
study. Was it the distribution of the learning trials that was critical,
or was it the fact that the initial learning of the $A-B$ list took
place on Monday? Did the temporal differentiation depend upon
the fact that $A-B$ learning was initiated on Monday and not upon
the fact that the acquisition trials on $A-B$ were distributed over
four days? The obvious next step was to have $A-B$ learned in its
entirety on Monday, with $A-D$ being learned on Thursday, and to
compare the recall of $A-D$ following this schedule with its recall
when $A-B$ and $A-D$ were both learned on Thursday. This step was
carried out by Underwood and Freund (1968), with the results
being depicted in Figure 6. With the Monday—Thursday schedule
for $A-B$ and $A-D$ learning, recall was 65%; with $A-B$ and $A-D$
both being learned on Thursday, recall was 38%. Although no
precise comparisons could be made with the previous work, it
seemed reasonable at the time to conclude that the distribution of
$A-B$ learning was not the critical independent variable; rather, it
was the temporal separation in the learning of the $A-B$ and $A-D$
lists that established the temporal discrimination.

The difference in the amount of forgetting over the 24 hours for
the two conditions shown in Figure 6 must be emphasized. In
another condition in the experiment, six of the 12 A-B pairs were
carried over intact into the $A-D$ list for the groups learning both
lists on Thursday. The recall of the six $A-D$ pairs not carried over
was essentially the same as for the condition in which both $A-B$
and $A-D$ learning occurred on Thursday. The purpose for carrying
over intact pairs was to make the temporal discrimination even
more difficult, assuming that such discrimination is based primarily
on information about list membership of the items. Although recall
was not influenced by the carryover of pairs, the number of intrusions (giving B responses at recall in place of D responses) was. In
fact, the number of correct responses and the number of intrusions
were about equal in frequency, and this implied that differentiation

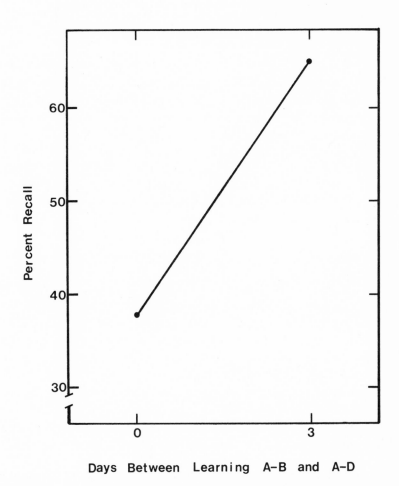

Days Between Learning A–B and A–D

FIGURE 6. Proactive interference as a function of the days separating the learning of $A-B$ and $A-D$. (Data from Underwood & Freund, 1968.)

was completely destroyed. We argued at that time that if the subject made a reasonable number of responses on the recall trial, the amount of proactive inhibition would never be much greater than that observed. Even with no temporal discrimination, if the subjects respond with some frequency to each stimulus term, they are likely to give the correct response for the $A-D$ list half the time.

SOME IMPLICATIONS

Our finding (as seen in Figure 6) was not an isolated one. Alin (1968) used serial lists of nonsense syllables. In one case, a six-day interval separated the learning of the two lists, and in another, the separation interval was 20 days. Recall was higher (proactive inhibition was less) for the latter condition than for the former. Ihalainen (1968) published an article in which four different experiments were reported on the influence of the interval between two intervening tasks on the recall of the second. His results, too, showed that several days between the two lists facilitated recall as compared with a few minutes between lists.

A criterion for evaluating the generality of a phenomenon of memory is whether it can be demonstrated also in a short-term memory paradigm. That is, can a buildup of proactive inhibition be retarded by inserting temporal intervals between the learning of successive interfering elements? At least three studies have shown this to be the case (Maslow, 1934; Peterson & Gentile, 1965; Kincaid & Wickens, 1970). It appears, therefore, that a fairly general conclusion may be reached, namely, that, as the interval between the acquisition of two potentially interfering lists increases, proactive inhibition decreases. Temporal differentiation, it seems, is a powerful deterrant to interfering processes.

Some of us have stated the extreme case of proactive inhibition, namely, that any associations learned from the beginning of life, which may be in apparent conflict with associations learned at any point in later life, will serve as a source of proactive inhibition for the later memory. But, speaking in relation to long-term proactive effects, we have seen that even a period as short as three days inserted between two interfering tasks ($A-B$ and $A-D$ lists) will essentially eliminate proactive interference. Are we then to change our thinking to correspond to such facts and conclude that proactive inhibition as a source of forgetting has been greatly overestimated? Are we to conclude that outside the laboratory, proactive inhibition is a minor factor in forgetting and that the potential of interference from early memories on later memories must be sharply restricted to memories that were established close together in time? Can a temporal differentiation be so powerful as to require such a change in thinking?

The unknown factor in the above reasoning is the length of the retention interval; that is, the interval between learning the second task and its recall. Logically, proactive inhibition, if there is to be any at all, must increase as some function of the length of the retention interval. We have seen that memory for the order of two events separated by a constant interval decreases as the interval increases after the second memory is established (Squire, Chace, & Slater, 1975). It would be anticipated that the temporal discrimination between two lists, established by having learned them on separate days, would decrease as the retention interval increases. In short, it would appear that we are dealing with two intervals that interact to produce changes in the magnitude of the proactive inhibition. If the temporal discrimination breaks down rather quickly as the retention interval increases, proactive inhibition could regain its status as a critical factor in forgetting.

It was apparent that an experiment was needed to resolve the issue, an experiment in which both of the intervals in question would be manipulated. For three years I delayed, hoping that some other investigator would see the need and undertake the work. The delay on my part was based on two matters. First, the outcome seemed logically to be foreordained; the two intervals simply had to interact in determining proactive inhibition. However, because I have seen a number of cases in our laboratory where results did not come out in a certain way when all logic, fact, and theory said they should, this presumed certainty of outcome alone was not a primary deterrant. But, when this was considered along with the second matter, I did pause. The fact is that such experiments are extremely difficult, expensive, and time consuming to do. It was, then, a question of where resources should be allocated. I do not remember the particular stimulus that made the decision; all I remember is that, at some point, I decided that the experiment simply had to be done. Simultaneously, the decision made was to do more than the bare-bones experiment necessary to show the interaction between the intervals.

EXPERIMENT 6

By all considerations, a Weber-like function should hold between temporal discrimination and the length of the interval between the two lists. This would imply that inserting a day between the learning of $A-B$ and the learning of $A-D$ would have a very strong effect, whereas, with each additional day inserted, the increase in the temporal discrimination should become less and less. This led us to use four intervals between the learning of $A-B$ and $A-D$, namely, 0, 1, 2, and 3 days. Three retention intervals were decided upon, 1, 4, and 8 days. We were, in fact, unable to carry out the conditions using the 8-day interval, and so only two retention intervals were involved. We had reason to believe that the results might be to some degree dependent upon the nature of the recall tests. If proactive inhibition results entirely from the failure of list discrimination, none should be found in an unpaced test in which list discrimination was not of moment. We therefore used two different types of retention tests for different groups of subjects: a paced recall of $A-D$ and an unpaced test, the latter being the MMFR test, in which the subject is asked to produce both the B and D response terms to each stimulus term, with no time pressure.

With 0, 1, 2, or 3 days separating $A-B$ and $A-D$ and with two retention intervals (1 day and 4 days), eight conditions were represented. In addition, two controls were used (one for each retention interval) in which only the $A-D$ list was learned. It can be seen that with two types of recall, a total of 20 different conditions was required. These 20 conditions were represented by 20 different groups of 18 subjects each.

Some Details

The $A-B$ list was learned either on Monday, Tuesday, Wednesday, or Thursday. The $A-D$ list was always learned on Thursday, and, for the groups learning $A-B$ on Thursday, $A-D$ learning followed immediately. Retention measurements were taken either on Friday (one-day retention interval) or on the following Monday (four-day retention interval).

The A-B and A-D lists consisted of 12 pairs. The words were all of two syllables and represented a random sample of a still larger random sample of two-syllable, AA words from Thorndike and Lorge (1944). All pairings were random, and one of the lists was arbitrarily designated as the $A-B$ list, the other as the $A-D$ list. The learning of $A-B$ was carried to one perfect trial using the anticipation method with the memory drum set at a 2:2-second rate. The $A-D$ learning was carried to the same criterion. On paced recall, the subjects were informed that they were to recall the second list of the two learned, to try to get as many correct on the first trial as possible, and then to continue until all responses were again correct on a single trial. The two control groups, C-1 and C-4, were merely asked to recall and relearn the single list $(A-D)$ they had learned.

The subjects in the groups given MMFR were provided with a sheet on which the stimulus terms were listed with two blanks after each. They were asked to write the response terms from the first list opposite the appropriate stimulus in the first column and to write the response terms for the second list in the second column. The test was unpaced, and the subjects were urged to guess when in doubt. The two control groups merely supplied the response terms for the $A-D$ list.

The 360 subjects were college students, assigned to particular conditions by a block-randomized schedule. Any subject requiring over 30 trials to reach the criterion on $A-B$ was dropped and replaced with the next subject by that particular experimentalist. The subjects were not allowed to serve in any other experiment while they were involved in the one under discussion.

The data-gathering phase of the experiment required approximately a year and a half and several durable and patient research assistants. Although I frequently scanned the raw data sheets during the course of testing, I only once made a tally of the recall, at a time when about half of the testing had been completed. Although I distinctly remember an unpleasant feeling attending these tallies, I quickly put it out of my mind with the rationalization that the subjects were too few in number to expect stable results at that time.

Results

A—B and A—D learning.   Sixteen groups learned the same $A—B$ list, four different groups on each of four different days. The groups would subsequently be differentiated on length of the retention interval and type of recall. The mean numbers of trials required to reach one perfect trial on the $A—B$ list were 12.64, 11.46, 11.25, and 12.54 for Monday, Tuesday, Wednesday, and Thursday, respectively. The first conclusion, of questionable profundity, is that day of the week is not related to rate of learning.

The mean numbers of trials to learn $A—D$ as a function of the day of the week (Monday through Thursday) on which $A—B$ was learned were 8.71, 8.14, 9.04, and 8.82. The four control groups averaged 9.19 trials to learn $A—D$, the means ranging between 8.44 and 9.81. Although the values for the control groups were somewhat greater than those for the experimental groups, the difference was not statistically reliable. The protocols were examined for intrusions of B terms during the learning of $A—D$, as a function of the temporal separation of the two lists. The number of subjects (out of 72 possible) contributing intrusions were 12, 11, 8, and 7 as the interval between $A—B$ and $A—D$ increased (0, 1, 2, 3 days). The corresponding total numbers of intrusions were 18, 22, 16, and 10.

The $A—B$ and $A—D$ lists were analyzed to determine the reliability of pair difficulty and the relationship between the difficulty of the $A—B$ pairs and the corresponding $A—D$ pairs. A rank was determined for each of the 12 $A—D$ pairs for 144 of the experimental subjects and an equivalent set of ranks for the remaining 144 experimental subjects. The correlation was .98, indicating very high reliability of pair difficulty. The correlation between the ranks for the $A—B$ pairs (summed across 288 subjects) and the ranks for the corresponding $A—D$ pairs (as determined by the stimulus identity) was .69. Clearly, the common stimulus terms in the two lists were substantially involved in determining pair difficulty in both lists.

Paced recall and relearning.   The number of correct $A—D$ responses on the paced recall trial were transformed to percents (using 12 as a base). These are shown in Figure 7. The dotted lines represent the recall for the two control groups (C-1 and C-4), and the solid lines the recall for the experimental groups (E-1 and E-4) after the same retention intervals. Although it is clear that there was heavy proactive inhibition in recall after both retention intervals, the unexpected finding is that the amount of proactive inhibition

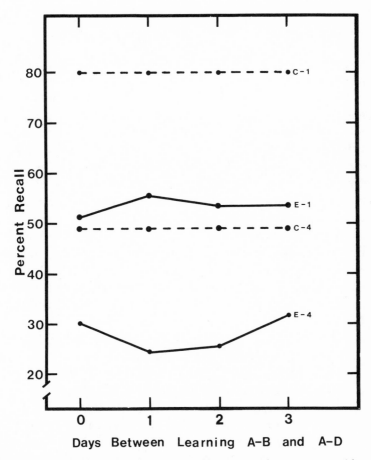

FIGURE 7. Paced recall as a function of the temporal separation and length of the retention interval. *C* refers to control groups (not having learned *A–B*) and *E* to the experimental groups. The number appended to *E* and *C* represents length of the retention interval in days (Experiment 6).

was unrelated to the temporal separation of $A-B$ and $A-D$; the recall was essentially invariant as a function of the day on which A-B was learned ($F = .12$). The essential results of the earlier study, which prompted the current one, were shown in Figure 6; the present results obviously fail to replicate the earlier finding that a difference of three days between $A-B$ and $A-D$ markedly reduced proactive interference. It has been said that experimental psychologists frequently have good reasons for demonstrating tendencies toward alcoholism; it is now evident as to why this might be true.

As may be seen in Figure 7, the amount of proactive inhibition (difference between E and C) appears to be about equivalent after one day and after four days, and this was supported by statistical tests. This means, therefore, that the proactive inhibition observed had reached its maximum within 24 hours after learning $A-D$. The relearning scores for $A-D$ (trials to reach one perfect) did not differ as a function of the interval between $A-B$ and $A-D$ learning for either retention interval, but there was clear evidence of proactive inhibition in relearning. The mean numbers of trials to relearn for Groups C-1 and C-4 were 2.78 and 3.78, respectively. For groups 0–1 and 0–4 (the two groups with a zero interlist interval during learning), the means were 3.83 and 4.44. An analysis of variance indicated that relearning was more rapid for the control groups than for the experimental groups, $F(1, 68) = 5.02, p < .05$, and that relearning was slower after the four-day interval than after the one-day interval ($F = 4.56$), but that the interaction was not reliable. In summary, the data yielded no evidence that a temporal separation between $A-B$ and $A-D$ produced a temporal differentiation, which in turn resulted in a reduction in proactive inhibition in paced recall. For all separations, the amount of proactive inhibition was statistically the same and, unlike most previous studies, the relearning was retarded by the proactive effects.

The degree of differentiation between lists has frequently been indexed by interlist intrusions during recall and relearning, with the greater number of intrusions being associated with low differentiation. For the groups having the one-day retention interval, the number of subjects producing intrusions and the total number of intrusions produced both decreased directly as the temporal separation between $A-B$ and $A-D$ increased. The numbers of subjects (out of a possible 18) producing intrusions were 13, 11, 7, and 3, for 0, 1, 2, and 3 days, respectively. The corresponding numbers of intrusions were 34, 21, 11, and 3. As indicated earlier, it was expected that, with a constant separation between A-B and A-D learning, the temporal discrimination between the two lists should decrease as the retention interval increased. The intrusions for the four-day retention interval support this expectation; however, the temporal separation in the learning of the two lists became a relatively minor factor at the four-day retention test. As the separation variable increased, the numbers of subjects producing intrusions were 14, 14, 12, and 12; the corresponding total numbers of intrusions were 31, 41, 25, and 25.

The intrusion data provided no obvious coherent picture relating recall and the temporal separation in the learning of $A-B$ and $A-D$. The intrusions (at the one-day interval) clearly indicated that intrusion likelihood and temporal separation were inversely related. Yet, recall was uninfluenced by the separation. Several points will be made about this situation.

1. To note a theoretical contradiction between recall and intrusions is not new (e.g., Underwood & Ekstrand, 1966); it raises the issue of whether intrusions are to be viewed as indices of an underlying causal factor in forgetting, or merely as concomitants of forgetting.

2. Intrusions may be epiphenominal in that across the separation variable there is a change in the criterion set by the subjects for responding with the B terms. With a long interval separating $A-B$ and $A-D$, a subject may realize that the B responses are not appropriate for the second-list recall; therefore he sets a high criterion for responding. With a short interval, this knowledge may not be present, and a lower criterion for responding may be set. In effect, this position asserts that there was a temporal discrimination that was directly related to the $A-B$, $A-D$ separation. But, if this was true, why was not recall influenced?

3. Another possibility is that the $A-B$ associations were forgotten over the interval, so that, with the three-day separation, there would

be fewer available responses to intrude than would be the case with the zero separation. Both in the present experiment and in experiments to be reported later, there is a great deal of evidence that would deny this position. For example, if this was the only factor involved, intrusions should be fewer in number after the four-day retention interval than after the one-day interval.

4. I think that, at this point, the most direct conclusion is that differential temporal coding of the two lists was not appreciably influenced by the separation between $A-B$ and $A-D$, and that the differences in the number of intrusions associated with the separation variable resulted from the criterion differences. These criterion differences (it may be conjectured) were associated with the relatively superficial knowledge that the lists had been learned on different days. The criterion established by the subject for responding decreased as the two lists learned were closer together in time. With the four-day retention interval, criterion differences were negligible.

MMFR. For this test, the subjects were given the 12 stimulus terms and were asked to supply the appropriate response terms in two columns, the first column for the B response terms, the second for the D terms. A stringent scoring procedure required that an item be counted correct only if paired with the appropriate stimulus in the appropriate list. The results for this type of scoring for the unpaced MMFR test are shown in Figure 8. Since $A-B$ was also recalled, a comparison between proactive and retroactive inhibition becomes possible.

At first glance, the data in Figure 8 appear to present a rather complicated picture. However, statistically the picture is relatively simple as far as the separation variable (days between $A-B$ and $A-D$) is concerned. All of the lines for both $A-B$ and $A-D$ may be considered to have zero slope, which means that the time between $A-B$ and $A-D$ did not influence the unpaced recall, $F(3, 136) = 2.52, p > .05$. Also, the separation variable did not interact with any of the other variables. Nevertheless, it might be argued that, in spite of the lack of statistical reliability, the fact that performance was better with the zero separation interval for all four cases cannot be completely ignored. If not to be ignored, it might be suggested that,

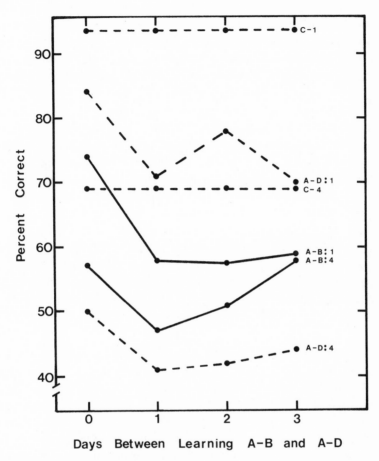

FIGURE 8. Unpaced recall (MMFR) for *A–B* and *A–D* when scored stringently in that an item was counted correct only if paired with the correct
stimulus in the appropriate list (Experiment 6).

again, criterion differences may lead to a greater number of responses
being produced with the zero separation than with the other separation intervals. The MMFR test does not guarantee that the subjects
will respond with all items available to them.

Figure 8 makes it evident that there were heavy losses in the
retention of both lists when the performance of the control groups
are used as reference points. Furthermore, although the *A–D* list

shows less loss after one day than does the $A-B$ list, the positions are reversed after the four-day retention interval. The statistical analysis for the eight experimental groups showed this interaction to be highly reliable (F = 33.27). In fact, if retention of $A-B$ is considered to reflect retroactive inhibition and the retention of $A-D$ to reflect proactive inhibition, and if the control groups are used as reference points, retroactive inhibition decreases as the retention interval increases, while proactive inhibition increases. This interaction obtains to a greater or lesser degree, regardless of the day on which A-B learning occurred. Perhaps most unexpected of all was the very heavy interference that occurred in the MMFR tests. Summing across the temporal separation variable and using the control groups as a base, proactive inhibition in MMFR was 18% after one day, and 25% after four days. The corresponding values for paced recall were 27% and 21%.

An evaluation was made of the MMFR results when the scoring was not stringent, that is, the criterion that the response terms must be in the appropriate list was eliminated. If proactive inhibition is largely a matter of the subject's inability to identify the appropriate list (first or second) for the response terms, it should have disappeared when this criterion for the scoring was eliminated. This was clearly not the case. Although performance on $A-D$ was higher than it was under stringent scoring, there was proactive inhibition for all eight groups. Again the separation variable had no reliable influence. The major consequence of reducing the stringency in scoring was to produce about equivalent amounts of retroactive and proactive inhibition after four days (approximately 58% recall versus 70% for the control). Finally, when the scoring involved only the production of response terms, the result was much the same as when only correct pairing was required. The number correct increased somewhat for all conditions, but again, proactive inhibition was evident in all eight conditions.

WHAT HAPPENED?

The failure to replicate one's own research does little to nourish the spirit. Even at my relatively advanced age, there were fleeting thoughts about joining my brother in his established business or about opening a small antique shop on the corner. In so doing, I would leave the whole bloody mess to my more stable colleagues at Berkeley, Stanford, Toronto, Oregon, and Colorado.

What had happened? After seeing the need for a carefully done parametric experiment to tie up the loose ends on the role of temporal coding in proactive inhibition, I waited three years before undertaking the needed experiment because the outcome seemed obvious and the costs were substantial. Finally, despairing that no one else had sufficient interest to do the study, it was done—and now the despair arose from another source. I had failed to replicate an effect, which by our usual standards was enormous. What had happened? It clearly was not a case in which nature had shown a fickle side; the results of the study were stable and orderly; they simply did not correspond to expectations based on previous results nor upon a crude theory of temporal coding. Most importantly, the results showed that a temporal code, different for each list, was not established by the procedures used. Or, if established, the differences in the temporal codes were insufficient to influence performance on either a paced or unpaced test of recall after 24 hours.

The experiment did produce evidence that proactive inhibition in the $A-B$, $A-D$ paradigm can occur in heavy amounts even with the MMFR test and that, in long-term memory, proactive interference may be as powerful or more powerful than retroactive interference. It is a very rare case to show proactive inhibition in relearning; clearly, the $A-B$ task exerted a strong effect on the recall and relearning of $A-D$, even when $A-B$ had been acquired eight days earlier. It was very tempting at this juncture to turn my attention to this topic (proactive inhibition) and forget about the central theme, namely, between-list temporal coding. It was not to be. I will leave the implications of the results of Experiment 6 for forgetting theory to another time. In following the central theme, I must face directly the reason for the failure to replicate earlier findings, but in doing so, proactive inhibition is seen primarily as a vehicle for the study of between-list temporal coding. In looking for possible reasons for the failure to reproduce the earlier result, attention must be directed toward static variables, which differed for the two experiments. One or more of these variables must interact with the interval between

A—B and *A—D* in determining performance. In assessing the likelihood of such an interaction for a given variable, the work of other investigators on between-list temporal coding becomes of some interest.

POTENTIAL INTERACTING VARIABLES

Lists

One of the obvious differences between our earlier experiment (1968) and the present one was in the lists used. Both sets of lists are shown in Table 2. For reference purposes, I will call the lists used in our earlier study the 1968 Lists, those in Experiment 6, the 1971 Lists. The 1968 Lists were used in a still earlier study on proactive inhibition, in which the major variables were degree of *A—B* learning and the massing or distribution of *A—B* learning (Underwood & Ekstrand, 1966). The three-letter words used as stimulus terms have relatively low and homogeneous frequency in the Thorndike-Lorge (1944) tables, the average frequency being approximately 13 per million. The two-syllable adjectives used as response terms varied widely in frequency, from 2 per million to one *AA* word. A rough average is 25 per million. The use of the one-syllable words as stimulus terms and the two-syllable words as response terms was intended to minimize the problem of discriminating between stimulus and response terms.

The words in the 1971 Lists were all of two syllable, *AA* frequency, and constituted a random sample of such words. Almost all of the words serve more than one function in the language. For example, the word *second* occurs as a noun, adjective, adverb, and verb. However, the most predominant usage of the 24 words is as nouns.

It may be asked why the 1968 Lists were not used for Experiment 6. The reason for not using the 1968 Lists was that some of the words from the lists were being used in another experiment being conducted at the same time as Experiment 6, and, since a subject might serve in both experiments, we did not want a repetition of words across experiments. It is this fortuitous set of events that

TABLE 2

Lists Used in the 1968 Study and in Experiment 6 (1971 Lists)

1968 Lists		1971 Lists	
A–B	*A–D*	*A–B*	*A–D*
cot–gloomy	cot–playful	listen–degree	listen–city
lid–absurd	lid–sturdy	outside–meeting	outside–army
elm–haughty	elm–angry	member–supply	member–fellow
tug–dirty	tug–barren	doctor–enjoy	doctor–question
mar–wicked	mar–lazy	daily–sudden	daily–human
bug–empty	bug–double	second–spirit	second–golden
kin–rural	kin–insane	modern–decide	modern–sugar
jaw–constant	jaw–frigid	market–island	market–herself
sly–fruitful	sly–healthy	single–heaven	single–suggest
ham–remote	ham–rotten	express–gentle	express–effort
gum–speedy	gum–cheerful	children–river	children–toward
wig–modest	wig–tranquil	uncle–honor	uncle–flower

surely must have changed the direction of our research for several years. I am convinced that, had we used the 1968 Lists for the 1971 experiment (Experiment 6), the results would have been as expected, and they would have shown a clear decreasing function between the amount of proactive interference and the days separating *A–B* and *A–D* learning. As it is, we have stumbled on some variable that has a rather profound effect on between-list discrimination. But whether this variable is one associated with list differences or is quite of a different nature remains to be seen. I have long believed that as a research strategy it is not a good idea to keep static variables constant across experiments when those variables are not of primary interest, and this is true in particular when the roles of the static variables are not understood. To hold static variables constant across experiments may prevent the discovery of critical interacting variables, and it may also prevent us from determining that some variables are irrelevant for a given phenomenon. In fact, however, I do not normally follow my own belief in this matter. It is easy and convenient to use the materials that are already available, to use the same length of list, to use the same intervals, and so on. It is quite apparent to me that had we been able to use the 1968 Lists in the 1971 experiment, we would have done so. Our lives would have been less jolted and restructured, but we very likely would not have made the discovery we have made, whatever it turns out to be.

A question concerning the choice of lists for the 1971 experiment still remains. Having found it necessary to construct new lists, why were the high-frequency words chosen? My notes do not give an answer to this question. Perhaps like the mountain, the random pool of two-syllable, *AA* words was there, and having no reason to believe that a critical choice was involved, I proceeded to use them.

Certainly one of the obvious differences between the two sets of lists is the frequency of the words. The 1971 Lists contain all *AA* words, whereas the 1968 Lists include a wide range of frequencies (although the stimulus terms are quite homogeneous with respect to this characteristic). Furthermore, it would seem that there is a theoretical reason why between-list differentiation might be more difficult as word frequency increases. It has been known since the work of Deese (1960) that high frequency words have more (and perhaps stronger) interitem associations than do low-frequency words. Thus, a word in *A—B* might be associated with a word in *A—D* (e.g., *human* and *spirit* in the 1971 Lists). Such associations might produce problems in establishing different temporal codes for the two lists. I have not found a directly relevant study on this matter, but a study by Winograd (1968a) is suggestive. He found that when words in two free-recall lists belonged to the same category, the subject was more likely to be wrong in list identification than was true when the words in the two lists did not belong to the same category. Interpreting the differences in the effect of temporal separation on proactive inhibition in terms of frequency differences for the two sets of lists, hence, differences in interitem associations, remains a possibility, but there are at least three arguments against such an interpretation.

1. In an earlier study (Underwood & Ekstrand, 1967), we tested the idea that, across successive lists, the proactive inhibition in 24-hour recall should build up more rapidly for lists of high-frequency words than for lists of low-frequency words. The reasoning was

exactly as indicated above, namely, that interlist associations among the high-frequency words should produce greater interference than would be present for the low-frequency words. The subjects learned four lists of paired associates, a 24-hour recall being given following the learning of each list and before the learning of the next list. We were not able to demonstrate a difference in the amount of proactive inhibition across successive lists for the low- and high-frequency words, although proactive inhibition did increase with each successive list.

2. Winograd (1968b) made a direct test of list differentiation as a function of word frequency using the free-recall format and two lists. He found that the identification of words with lists was poorer for high-frequency words than for low-frequency words on an immediate test. However, if level of identification was equated for the two frequency levels on an immediate test, there was no difference in the number of errors on identification after 24 hours.

3. Even if we grant that word frequency may be involved to some degree in the differences in the results for the 1968 and 1971 Lists, it is difficult to see how the temporal separation in Experiment 6 could be so utterly without influence on performance, if distinctive temporal codes for $A-B$ and $A-D$ were established. Surely, if they were established, we would expect some residue for the groups having three days separating the learning of $A-B$ and $A-D$. To suppose that differentiating temporal codes were established but completely lost within 24 hours remains a possibility, but if this is true, temporal coding becomes of little consequence for long-term retention.

Are there other differences in the characteristics of the words in the 1968 and 1971 Lists that might be involved in producing the puzzle? There is the obvious difference in the ability of the subject to discriminate between stimulus and response terms in the lists, but I have not been able to go from this to an account of the results. There is still another difference, which is suggestive. Evidence from the work of Hicks and Young (1973) suggests that subjects may be better able to discriminate among adjectives in two successive free-recall lists than to discriminate among lists of nouns. A distinction between adjectives and nouns as response terms has some validity in distinguishing between the 1968 Lists and the 1971 Lists. Still, in our 1968 study, we were able to destroy almost completely the discrimination between the two lists (with adjectives as response terms) when some of the $A-B$ pairs were carried over to the $A-D$ list, a procedure which approximates the one used in the Hicks-Young study.

At this point in our research, I could not find evidence that seemed at all convincing that the differences in the results of the two experiments were tied to the differences in the characteristics of the words used to construct the lists. Knowing that words differ on so many different characteristics, I could not but feel a lack of confidence in this conclusion.

Level of $A-B$ Learning

In the 1968 study, the subjects were given 32 anticipation trials on $A-B$; in the 1971 study, the subjects were carried to one perfect trial on $A-B$. The difference in the number of trials was about 3 to 1; level of learning on $A-B$ in the 1968 study was far higher than the level in Experiment 6. The decision to carry $A-B$ to a relatively low level of learning for Experiment 6 was made on the basis of previous evidence (Underwood & Ekstrand, 1966), indicating that, beyond a relatively low level of $A-B$ learning, proactive inhibition did not increase as the number of trials on $A-B$ learning increased. I do not remember why we used 32 trials in the 1968 study because the reasoning applied to the 1971 study could have been as well applied to the 1968 study. Having done what we have done, the question is whether or not the villain variable is the level of $A-B$ learning. That the level of $A-B$ learning is not a critical variable was a conclusion reached using the 1968 Lists; we must face the possibility that level of learning as a variable may be tied to particular lists.

Is level of learning a factor in studies of list discrimination? The answer is decidedly "yes," although as Abra (1972) has pointed out, the problems of measurement and other problems do not make this variable a neat one with which to work. One problem involves relative strength of the items between two (or more) lists as related to the absolute strength in either list. Nevertheless, in what may be a simplified conclusion, it seems that both relative and absolute strength (defined in terms of number of trials) enter into decisions as to the list membership of a given item on tests for list differentiation (e.g., Abra, 1970; Hintzman & Waters, 1970; Winograd, 1968c).

Assume that, as in the 1968 study, there was a large difference in the number of trials given $A-B$ and $A-D$. How could such a difference mediate a temporal discrimination? There seems to be two possibilities. First, the greater the number of trials the greater the span of time over which a temporal code (however acquired) might persist as an $A-B$ code. Second, number of trials per se might be used as a discriminative cue between the $A-B$ and $A-D$ list. For example, in the 1968 study, the $A-B$ response terms may have been associated with the list given many, many trials, while $A-D$ response terms were associated with the list given relatively few trials. This is to say that a frequency discrimination serves as the basis for differentiating the two sets of response terms. There is some indirect evidence that, with a relatively small number of trials, such a discrimination is possible and, when possible, reduces proactive interference (Underwood & Ekstrand, 1968, Experiments III and IV). If frequency-discrimination differences are responsible for the present puzzle, the reasoning about them might be somewhat as follows: In the 1968 study, the numbers of trials on $A-B$ and $A-D$ were 32 and 12 (roughly); in Experiment 6, the learning of both $A-B$ and $A-D$ was carried to one perfect trial, the means being roughly 12 trials and 8 trials, respectively. The former difference might well be discriminable on the basis of frequency; the latter difference might not. The problem with this type of explanation is that there must be some concomitant assumption about frequency discriminations as a function of the temporal separation. In effect, the assumption would be that, when two lists are learned in immediate succession, the frequency discrimination breaks down as a means of differentiating the response terms in the two lists, whereas, if the two lists are separated by several days, it does not break down. This does not seem to be a reasonable assumption; indeed, the opposite assumption would appear to be a better one, but it would simply not mediate the 1968 results.

Without much theoretical or empirical backing, it can be said that it is possible that the number of trials on $A-B$ may in some way interact with the type of words used to construct the lists and that, as a consequence, the effect of a temporal separation between $A-B$ and $A-D$ on proactive interference will only emerge when $A-B$ learning is carried to a far higher level than was true in Experiment 6. An experiment to test this possibility will be reported as the first experiment in the next chapter.

Other Findings

With only one exception, the studies on establishing temporal codes—on list differentiation—have used the basic method as given in Experiment 3, described in Chapter 1. That is, free-recall lists have been the major vehicle. Furthermore, the number of learning trials on the items has been low, relative to the number of trials we are dealing with in the experiments that got us enmeshed in the present puzzle. Although we might like to believe that principles of temporal coding should supercede any particular type of task or level of learning, our ignorance on such matters is such as to lead to caution. The puzzle we are dealing with concerns lists forming the $A-B$, $A-D$ paradigm, and the lists were given many learning trials. The one study that used this paradigm and asked directly about list differentiation was performed by McCrystal (1970). His materials were very similar to those used in the 1968 Lists. The stimulus terms were high-association value nonsense syllables and the response terms were two-syllable adjectives. The learning of both $A-B$ and $A-D$ learning was carried to one perfect trial in immediate succession. List differentiation tests were given at five different intervals up to seven days. For the test of list differentiation, the subjects were given the response terms from the two lists, one at a time, and were allowed 12 seconds to make a decision concerning the list membership. The largest decline in correct identification occurred over the first 20 minutes following the learning of $A-D$. After this, the decline was very gradual up to seven days, but even at seven days performance was clearly above chance. McCrystal points out, however, that, with time, a measurement problem may lead to an underestimation of the loss of differentiation. His reasoning is that over time, if forgetting occurs, guessing becomes more and more prominent and that, therefore, the number correct for the longer retention intervals is more influenced by guessing than is the number correct at the short retention intervals.

One possible interpretation of Experiment 6 (mentioned earlier) is that, for these lists, the loss of differentiation over time proceeds very quickly and that, even with a three-day separation between $A-B$ and $A-D$, differentiation is completely lost within the 24-hour period. The gradual decline shown by McCrystal would certainly not support this notion, even for lists learned in immediate succession. But caution still must prevail; it remains a possibility that the characteristics of the 1971 Lists are such that loss of differentiation is extremely rapid, and that the lack of differences in recall at 24 hours for the different separations between $A-B$ and $A-D$ reflects this rapid loss.

In Chapter 1, I pointed out the powerful influence of recency of stimulation for limiting the response attempts to the appropriate response pool. It should be fairly evident that had the retention interval for the paced recall of $A-D$ in Experiment 6 been a minute or two, there probably would have been little proactive inhibition. Just how long the recency principle extends in time is not known, although McCrystal's study suggests a fairly rapid drop initially. I think that this mechanism should be kept quite separate from what I have called differential temporal coding of two lists. When the memories for two lists are differentiated by temporal coding, it is presumably accomplished by mechanisms discussed in Chapter 2. I have viewed the results of Experiment 6 as indicating that differentiating temporal codes for the two lists were not established, or if so, were completely lost within 24 hours. A study using a short retention interval, for example, 30 minutes, would seem to be indicated. For two reasons, such an experiment was not done. First, even if the temporal separation of $A-B$ and $A-D$ was found to be associated with differences in recall, the interpretation would be unclear because such a difference might be produced by a recency principle rather than by differential temporal coding of the two lists. Second, the basic puzzle between the two experiments would remain: Why would temporal codes for the 1968 and 1971 Lists be lost at different rates?

There is one final matter. In discussing the design of Experiment 6, I made it clear that I believed there were two intervals of importance in determining the amount of differentiation between lists, namely, the $A-B$ to $A-D$ interval and the retention interval following the learning of $A-D$. Insofar as proactive interference is determined by loss of list differentiation, one can be predicted from the other. It seems fair to say that the most general interpretation of proactive inhibition rests squarely on loss of temporal codes for the lists, and the two intervals in question are the critical ones for determining loss. Hintzman and Waters (1969) varied these two intervals using two unrelated lists presented for one trial each. The outcome was as expected; with 15 minutes between the presentation of the two lists, differentiation was better both immediately and after 51 minutes than when the two lists were not separated by an interval in presentation. Over 24 hours, the advantage of the separation disappeared. Correct list identification fell to about 55% after 24 hours, whereas (disregarding the separation variable) it was approximately 65% on the immediate test. In concluding their report, Hintzman and Waters indicate that their results strongly support current theoretical accounts of forgetting, with particular reference to proactive inhibition; proactive inhibition is due to loss of information concerning list membership. To attribute some proactive interference to a learning deficit of $A-D$ may be appropriate (e.g., Hasher & Johnson, 1975), but certainly the loss of temporal codes over time is of basic importance.

THE PUZZLE SUMMARIZED

Two experiments have given quite different outcomes with respect to the role of temporal coding in proactive interference. In examining these two experiments, two different static variables have been identified as possibly being involved in the interaction, namely, the characteristics of the words making up the lists and the level of $A-B$ learning. There were, of course, other identifiable differences in the conditions for the two studies. The data were collected in different years and by different experimenters. The research assist-ants who supervised the data collection differed. The subjects giving us the data differed. We must assume that such factors are not responsible for the puzzle; to assume otherwise would make the task of solving it hopeless. As we will see, hopelessness is not without some meaning, even when dealing with variables which might rea-sonably be involved.

4
The Chase

In this chapter, several experiments will be reported that were conducted in an effort to discover reasons why the 1968 study showed that proactive interference was sharply related to the length of the interval between learning $A-B$ and $A-D$, whereas no relationship was found in Experiment 6. It will be seen that there was a certain amount of thrashing around as attempts were made to develop new techniques for examining temporal coding differences.

EXPERIMENT 7

The first experiment was an examination of the effect of the level of $A-B$ learning. In the 1968 study, the $A-B$ learning was carried for 32 anticipation trials, whereas, in Experiment 6, the learning of $A-B$ was carried until each subject achieved a perfect performance (about 12 trials). In Experiment 7, the 1971 Lists were used with $A-B$ learning carried for 32 anticipation trials. The temporal separation between learning $A-B$ and learning $A-D$ was either zero days or 3 days. A paced recall test for $A-D$ was given either 1 day or 4 days following $A-D$ learning.

Method

The above design required four groups of subjects identified as 0–1, 0–4, 3–1, and 3–4; the first number refers to the number of days between learning $A-B$ and learning $A-D$, and the second number refers to the length of the retention interval in days. All procedures were exactly the same as those used in Experiment 6 for the paced-recall groups, except that, for all four conditions, the $A-B$ list was presented for one study trial followed by 32 anticipation trials. The four conditions were block randomized and 18 subjects were assigned to each.

Results

A—B and A—D learning.   During the 32 *A—B* learning trials, 70 of the 72 subjects attained one perfect trial. The two remaining subjects were arbitrarily assigned a value of 32 trials and the mean number of trials required to reach one perfect trial was determined. The means for the four groups varied between 10.94 and 14.39 trials, and did not differ statistically. The overall mean (12.67) was quite comparable to that reported for Experiment 6, where the mean for the 16 groups was 11.97 trials. Across the 32 *A—B* trials, the number of correct anticipations of the total possible averaged 83%. The mean number of trials required to reach the criterion of one perfect trial on *A—D* varied between 7.10 and 9.22 trials, with the means not being statistically different for the four groups. Again, these values were quite comparable to those obtained in Experiment 6.

Recall   Figure 9 shows the percentage recall for the four groups plotted as a function of the separation of *A—B* and *A—D* and as a function of the retention interval. Changing the level of *A—B* learning did not change the conclusion concerning the separation variable given by Experiment 6. Although there is a slight slope to the line depicting the Friday recall, an analysis of variance showed that only the retention interval produced a reliable effect on performance ($F = 24.18$); all other Fs were less than unity. Differences in relearning reflected the differences in recall.

A word of caution is in order about interpreting the absolute level of recall in all of the experiments involving the basic methods of Experiments 6 and 7. In an ideal world all subjects assigned to such an experiment would be naive to laboratory studies of verbal learning. This prevents associations learned by the subjects in previous laboratory experiments from becoming sources of interference in recall. As a practical matter, conducting experiments with this restriction is very difficult within the system used in our laboratory. As a part of the course requirement for introductory psychology, students must get a certain amount of experience as laboratory subjects. To require that subjects be serving in their first experiment when they contract

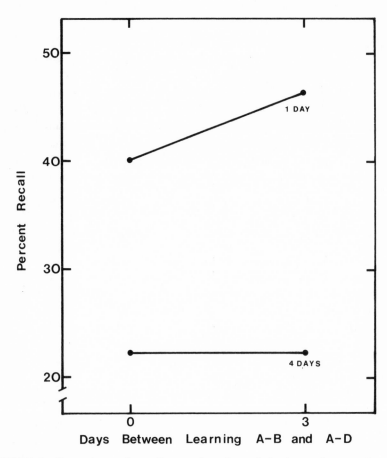

FIGURE 9. Percentage of recall as a function of the interval separating the learning of $A-B$ and $A-D$ and as a function of the retention interval (1 day and 4 days) (Experiment 7).

for experiments would essentially mean that naive subjects could only be obtained during the first week or two of the school term. To carry out the present experiments under the ideal conditions would have required many years. Therefore, we have set only the requirement that a subject must not serve in a different experiment during the period required to complete an experiment such as Experiment 7. This removes retroactive interference from other experiments as a source of forgetting, but it does not remove pro-active interference from previous experiments as a source. The upshot of this is that the differences in level of recall among the various experiments cannot readily be interpreted. For example, recall after 24 hours in Experiment 6 is somewhat higher than in the present experiment. This might be due to differences in the level of $A-B$ learning, but it is more probably that it is due to differences in experimental backgrounds of the subjects used in the two experiments. For present purposes, the critical finding lies in the slope of the recall curves. We have concluded that, in Experiment 7, the slope of these curves did not change as the level of $A-B$ learning was changed from approximately 12 trials (Experiment 6) to 32 trials (Experiment 7).

The numbers of intrusions of the B terms during the recall and relearning of $A-D$ were again shown to be related to temporal separation. The numbers observed were 44, 24, 5, and 30 for conditions 0–1, 0–4, 3–1, and 3–4, respectively.

EXPERIMENT 8

It was concluded that the results of Experiment 7 eliminated level of $A-B$ learning as a possible cause for the discrepancy between the results of the 1968 experiment and those of Experiment 6. What next? In view of the two potential interacting variables discussed in the previous chapter, having eliminated the level of $A-B$ learning, the differences in the characteristics of the words making up the lists might have become the next candidate for pursuit. I chose a different alternative at this point. This resulted in part from the fact that I had not yet seen a convincing way to attack the list-difference variable and in part from the fact that a completely new possibility began to nag at me.

The critical data in the 1968 study were based on a difference between two groups of subjects. It is true that other conditions in the experiment fit conceptually into the basic finding. It is true also that studies using the distribution of $A-B$ learning over several days had produced almost precisely the same quantitative results as found in the 1968 study, where all $A-B$ learning occurred on a single day. It was my interpretation that the same outcome for the distribution of $A-B$ trials and the separation of $A-B$ and $A-D$ both resulted from a common mechanism, namely, high differentiation of the temporal codes for the two interfering lists. This interpretation could be incorrect; the distribution of $A-B$ and the separation of $A-B$ and $A-D$ by three days may have produced the same essential outcome for quite different reasons. However, if the two sets of results occurred for quite different reasons, the basic puzzle confronting us still remained because of a contradiction between the results for two groups of subjects in 1968 and the results for the many groups involved in Experiment 6.

Many, many experiments are conducted in our laboratory, both by faculty and by graduate students. Most of the experiments use random-group designs. If the statisticians are correct on the matter, we would expect periodically a statistical miscarriage, in which reliable differences occurred by chance. Could the results for the two groups depicted in Figure 6 of Chapter 3 have been the results of such a miscarriage? This was a debilitating idea, but when strength returned, the necessary experiment was conducted.

Method

The purpose of Experiment 8 was to conduct a replication of the two-group, 1968 study. In the 1968 study two groups had 32 trials on $A-B$. Then, one group waited three days before learning $A-D$, while the other group learned $A-D$ immediately. For both groups, recall of $A-D$ was taken after 24 hours. For Experiment 8, we duplicated the conditions for these two groups as closely as we possibly could, using, of course, the 1968 Lists. My research assistant at the time, Charles S. Reichardt, proposed a possibility that led to our testing two additional groups. Suppose that the entire puzzle resulted from unusual characteristics of the particular words of the 1968 Lists. Even if we could replicate the 1968 study, it would not be strong evidence for the generality of the finding. Reichardt's proposal was that we construct another set of lists having the same general structure as the 1968 Lists but differing in terms of the particular words employed. Such wisdom could not be ignored, and so a second set of lists was constructed—Set 2, as opposed to the original set, which will be called Set 1. Three-letter words were used as stimulus terms, and they had an average Thorndike-Lorge (1944) frequency of 14 per million. The response terms were, as in Set 1, two-syllable adjectives with heterogeneous frequencies averaging about 19 per million.

To summarize: Four groups of 18 subjects each were used. Two of the groups learned the $A-B$ and $A-D$ lists identified as Set 1; two learned Set 2. Two groups learned $A-B$ on Monday for 32 anticipation trials; two groups learned $A-B$ on Thursday. All groups learned $A-D$ on Thursday (to one perfect trial), with recall and relearning of $A-D$ occurring 24 hours later.

Results

A—B and A—D learning.   All subjects attained one perfect trial on $A-B$ within the 32-trial limit imposed. The mean numbers of trials required to attain this criterion were 8.67 and 10.06 for the two groups learning Set 1, and 13.50 and 11.28 for the two groups learning Set 2. An analysis showed that the $A-B$ list from Set 2 was more difficult than the corresponding list from Set 1, $F(1, 68)$ = 4.51, $p < .05$. The difference in the difficulty of the sets was also observed in the proportion of correct responses given across the 32 trials, averaging 88% for Set 1 and 83% for Set 2.

Differences in set difficulty were likewise evident in learning $A-D$. For Set 1, the two means representing the numbers of trials to reach one perfect trial were 7.00 and 7.83, while, for Set 2, the values were 11.44 and 10.56. The difference was reliable, $F(1, 68) = 7.69, p < .01$. No reason for the differences in difficulty of the two sets was found. Nevertheless, because of the differences in difficulty, it could be argued that the results have greater generality than would have been the case if differences in difficulty were not present.

Recall   The percent recall of $A-D$ for each of the four groups is plotted as Figure 10. It is quite apparent that recall is better with the temporal separation between the learning of $A-B$ and $A-D$ than without such separation, and this is true for both sets of lists. The

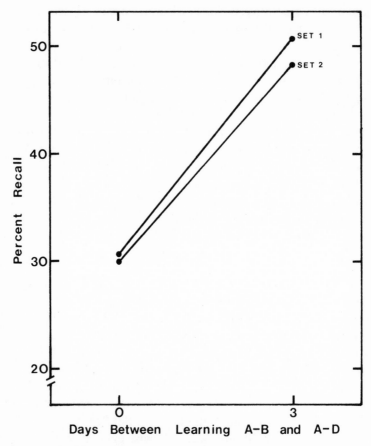

FIGURE 10.   Recall as a function of days separating $A-B$ and $A-D$ learning of two sets of lists (Experiment 8).

temporal variable was the only reliable source of variance (F = 13.69). We must conclude that the original 1968 finding was not the result of a statistical fluke; the present findings in general are the same as the original finding, although level of recall is lower in the present experiment, and the slope of the curves is somewhat less.

The number of trials to relearn did not differ among the four groups. As in the previous experiments, the number of intrusions of B terms in the recall and relearning of $A-D$ was far less with the long temporal separation than with the zero separation. For Set 1, the total numbers were 13 and 61, and, for Set 2, they were 6 and 52.

EXPERIMENT 9

Experiment 7 demonstrated that the differences in the results for the 1968 study and Experiment 6 were not due to different levels of $A-B$ learning. Experiment 8 showed that the 1968 result was repeatable. It would seem, therefore, that if the chase was to continue, the logic indicated that attention must be focused on the differences in the characteristics between the 1968 Lists and the 1971 Lists. But logic and reality are sometimes at odds. What characteristics of the lists could be responsible? There are multiple differences between the lists. An attempt to trace their implications by constructing new lists, which emphasized high and low levels of each characteristic, and then putting these lists to experimental test would, to say the least, be very time consuming. Furthermore, even if such a series of experiments were successful in identifying one or two presumable critical factors, the outcome would be less pointed than it might seem. Anyone who has sought to filter out a unidimensional task variable underlying a given phenomenon knows the frustration that attends the effort. The various characteristics of words may be given presumed independent definitions by various scaling procedures, but are still usually found to be quite highly correlated. It becomes impossible to determine the influence of one characteristic without contamination by at least one other. The logic of the puzzle that confronted me indicated that the answer must lie somewhere in the differences in the characteristics of the words in the two sets of lists, but I resolved not to be caught in the word-characteristic trap, even if it required abandoning the chase. No only would such a pursuit lead into the Geritol years, but even a favorable outcome would lead to a conclusion such as: "Temporal differentiation in an interference paradigm differs as a function of the adjectivalness of the words in the lists or some characteristic(s) associated with adjectivalness."

Believing that the evidence pointed to differences in task characteristics as the cause of the puzzle, yet choosing not to pursue the matter at this level, obviously posed a dilemma. Yet, there were ways to attack the problem without getting involved in the characteristics of the words per se. For example, perhaps the critical difference between the two sets of lists lies in the differences in discriminability of the stimulus and response terms, this discriminability being high in the 1968 Lists and low in the 1971 Lists. The effect of this variable could be examined without concern for the characteristics of the words. I was unable to develop a reasonable theoretical reason as to why the discriminability of stimulus and response terms should have such a profound influence on temporal coding, and, at this point in time, preferred not to study this variable.

Another line of research in our laboratory was indicating to us that unlearning differences in the $A-B$, $A-D$ paradigm were in some way related to the form class of the words used in the lists. By unlearning, of course, I mean the loss of information about items and associations in the $A-B$ list immediately after the learning of $A-D$. In Experiment 9, therefore, we asked about differences in unlearning between the 1968 Lists and the 1971 Lists. The thinking was that if we could find another phenomenon associated differentially with the two sets of lists, the analytical steps might be much easier to take than those required in studying the separation variable. Furthermore, it was known that lack of discriminability between lists in the $A-B$, $A-D$ paradigm did influence the amount of unlearning. It seemed, therefore, that a test of unlearning might be important in directing subsequent experiments designed to resolve the puzzle.

Method

Two groups of 18 subjects each were assigned randomly, one to the 1968 Lists, and one to the 1971 Lists. The $A-B$ and $A-D$ learning, which occurred in immediate succession, was carried to one perfect recitation, using the anticipation method and a 2:2-second rate. Immediately after learning $A-D$, the subjects were given an unpaced MMFR test in which they were requested to produce the response terms from both lists and assign them to the appropriate stimulus terms, placing them in one column for the first list and in another column for the second list.

Results

For the first time, Experiment 9 supplied valid information on the relative difficulty in learning the two sets of lists. The mean numbers of trials required to learn $A-B$ and $A-D$ from the 1968 Lists were 8.50 and 6.75, respectively. For the 1971 Lists, the corresponding values were 13.22 and 7.33. For $A-B$ and $A-D$ combined, the 1971 Lists were more difficult than were the 1968 Lists, $F(1, 34) = 4.93$, $p < .05$. Differences in learning $A-B$ and $A-D$ were clearly apparent ($F = 28.80$) for both sets of lists, but the interpretation is unclear because the $A-B$ and $A-D$ lists were not counterbalanced and may differ in intrinsic difficulty. It is of some importance to note that the mean number of trials required to learn the $A-D$ list was approximately the same for both sets of lists. This means that the interval between the end of learning $A-B$ and the MMFR test was about the same for both sets.

The performance on the MMFR test was scored stringently (correct pairing and correct list). For the 1968 Lists, the mean for $A-B$ was 9.28 and, for the 1971 Lists, 8.61 ($F < 1$). Recall of $A-D$ was essentially perfect for both lists (11.67 and 11.83). The conclusion was clear; these two sets of lists did not produce differences in unlearning, and the attempt to discover another phenomenon associated with the lists was judged to be unsuccessful in this experiment.

EXPERIMENT 10

In reporting the results of Experiment 6, in which the 1971 Lists were used, it was noted that the difficulty of the $A-B$ pairs was substantially correlated with the difficulty of the corresponding $A-D$ pairs ($r = .69$). This correlation was calculated by first summing the number of correct responses (across subjects) for each $A-B$ pair and independently summing for each $A-D$ pair. The correlation held between the 12 $A-B$ scores, and the 12 $A-D$ scores aligned by the common stimulus terms. Although not reported earlier, this same relationship was observed in Experiment 7, the correlations varying between .56 and .80 for the four groups. One implication is that the stimulus terms in the 1971 Lists are primarily involved in determining pair difficulty; the response term plays a less prominent role.

We examined the experiments in which the 1968 Lists had been used to determine the role of the stimulus terms on pair difficulty. In Experiment 8, the correlations for the two groups given Set 1 were .28 and .29. In Experiment 9, the correlation was −.11 (in the same experiment, the correlation for the 1971 Lists was .63). These correlations (.28, .29, −.11) may be considered zero, statistically. Without presenting the evidence, we will simply assert that this lack of relationship is not due to the lack of reliability in item difficulty. It may also be noted that the lists called Set 2 in Experiment 8 (constructed in the same manner as the 1968 Lists but using different words) showed the same lack of relationship in the difficulty of $A-B$ and $A-D$ pairs. It appeared, therefore, that the response terms for the 1968 Lists were largely responsible for pair difficulty whereas the stimulus terms were largely responsible for pair difficulty in the 1971 Lists. Is this difference between the lists responsible for the puzzle? In this case, it was possible to work out a theory to explain why this difference between the 1968 and 1971 Lists could produce the different findings in proactive interference, as a function of the temporal separation of $A-B$ and $A-D$ learning. The reasoning behind the theory was somewhat tortuous, and, in view of the fact that the experiment did not provide us with the necessary evidence to support it, I will keep the presentation at the empirical level.

As described, the item correlations for the 1968 Lists indicated that the response terms (two-syllable adjectives) largely determined pair difficulty, with the stimulus terms (three-letter words) contributing much less. Now, suppose we turn these lists over and use the two-syllable adjectives as stimulus terms and the three-letter words as response terms. If the reasoning has been sound concerning the source of item difficulty, the first expectation is that the correlation between $A-B$ and $A-D$ pair difficulty should increase substantially. This follows because the two-syllable adjectives determine pair difficulty, and, in the turned-over version, the two-syllable adjectives become the A terms in both lists.

If the first expectation is realized in the data, the lists will now become like the 1971 Lists in terms of the source of pair difficulty for $A-B$ and $A-D$. And, if this represents a critical difference between the 1968 and 1971 Lists, the 1968 Lists should now behave like the 1971 Lists. This is to say that the temporal separation between $A-B$ and $A-D$ learning should become irrelevant to proactive inhibition in recall.

Method

The stimulus (A) terms for the $A-B$ and $A-D$ lists were the two-syllable adjectives used as the response terms (B) in the 1968 $A-B$ list (see table in previous chapter). The response terms for $A-B$ were the three-letter words used as stimulus terms in Set 2 of Experiment 8. The response terms for the $A-D$ list were the three-letter words used as stimulus terms in the 1968 Lists.

Two groups of 20 subjects each were assigned to the two conditions, these conditions differing only in the length of the temporal separation (0 and 3 days) between $A-B$ and $A-D$ learning. The Monday—Thursday schedule for $A-B$ and $A-D$ was used for the three-day separation, and both lists were learned in immediate succession on Thursday for the zero separation. Recall and relearning of $A-D$ occurred on Friday, 24 hours following its learning. The learning of $A-B$ consisted of 32 anticipation trials, with $A-D$ learning carried to one perfect trial. The other details of the procedure were the same as in the previous experiments.

Results

The group learning $A-B$ on Monday required 15.15 trials to reach on perfect trial, and all except one of the 20 subjects reached this criterion within 32 trials. For $A-D$ learning on Thursday, 9.65 trials were required to attain one perfect trial. For the group learning both $A-B$ and $A-D$ on Thursday, the mean numbers of trials to reach one perfect on $A-B$ and $A-D$ were 12.55 and 10.30 respectively. An analysis showed that only the difference between learning $A-B$ and $A-D$ was reliable statistically. For the group with the three-day separation between $A-B$ and $A-D$ learning, the correlation between the number of correct responses for the $A-B$ pairs and the number correct for the corresponding $A-D$ pairs was .50. For the group having no separation between $A-B$ and $A-D$ learning, the value was .31. It had been anticipated that $A-B$ and $A-D$ item correlations would increase when the two-syllable adjectives became the stimulus terms. It is apparent that they did increase, but not to the level of the 1971 Lists. (.69), and neither would be judged significantly different from zero by conventional tests. On this matter, then, the results are somewhat ambiguous.

The recall results are shown in Figure 11. Again, the three-day separation produced a considerable influence on recall. The difference between the two groups was reliable, $F(1, 38) = 8.88, p < .01$, and the magnitude of the difference is almost exactly the same as found in Experiment 8, as exhibited in Figure 10. The difference

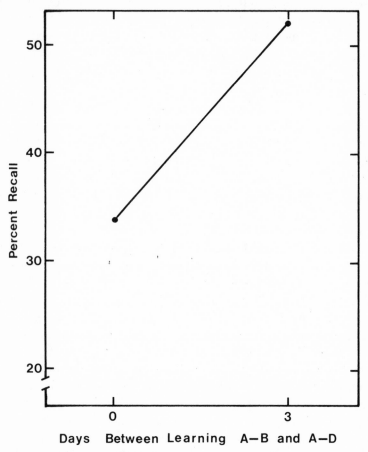

FIGURE 11.   Percent recall as a function of the interval separating $A-B$ and $A-D$ learning (Experiment 10).

in relearning (4.65 trials and 3.80 trials) $A-D$ to one perfect trial reflected the differences in recall but was not statistically reliable. With the three-day separation in learning the two lists, there were only 8 intrusions in recall and relearning, whereas, with the zero interval between the two lists, the intrusions totaled 57.

It must be concluded that the use of the turned-over versions of the 1968 Lists has changed nothing fundamentally; the effect of the temporal separation for these lists cannot be said to have been influenced by switching the position of the stimulus and response terms.

ECONOMY STEPS WHICH FAILED

Techniques for studying short-term memory have the potential of exhibiting the phenomena of long-term memory, and, in so doing, they can reduce days to minutes and hours to seconds. It was quite natural that we should turn to the use of short-term techniques in our chase. Indeed, it sometimes seemed that such a move was absolutely necessary if we were going to be able to look back on the decade of the seventies as one in which we had made some headway toward understanding the source of the puzzle, a puzzle that seemed to have gained functional autonomy as a driving force in our research. Among the various short-term memory techniques we tried, two were found to be procedurally sound, and a sufficient number of subjects was tested to determine the outcomes.

The first approach was to see if we could reproduce the basic findings exhibited by the 1968 Lists. The $A-B$ list was given for a study trial and a single anticipation trial, the pairs being presented at a 4:4-second rate. The $A-D$ list was given in precisely the same way. There were two groups. For one group, $A-D$ learning followed immediately the learning of $A-B$; for the other group, a five-minute interval was inserted between the learning of the two lists. The retention interval (time between $A-D$ learning and its recall) was 5 minutes for both groups. Ten subjects were tested under each of the two conditions. The subjects worked on the pyramid puzzle during the five-minute intervals.

The mean numbers of correct anticipations in learning were 7.2 and 7.9 for $A-B$ and $A-D$, respectively, for the group with no interval between $A-B$ and $A-D$ learning. For the group with the five-minute interval between $A-B$ and $A-D$ learning, the corresponding means were 6.2 and 7.7. After 5 minutes, $A-D$ recall averaged 8.9 correct responses, when there was no interval between the learning of $A-B$ and $A-D$, and 8.8 when the interval was 5 minutes. Thus, there was no evidence that proactive interference was reduced with the temporal separation of $A-B$ and $A-D$.

In the second study a procedure patterned after the Brown-Peterson technique was employed. The subjects were presented the $A-B$ pair for 1 second, followed by the $A-D$ pair for 1 second, followed by backward number counting for 20 seconds. At the end of the 20-second period, the subjects were asked to recall either the first pair presented $(A-B)$ or the second pair $(A-D)$. The subjects were fully informed as to the requirements. Each subject was given 24 pairs of pairs, these being the $A-B$ and $A-D$ pairs from the 1968 and 1971 Lists. The pairs from the two lists were ordered randomly. A further random order was constructed for the recall requirements such that, on half of the tests, the subjects were asked to recall $A-B$ (the first pair shown) and, on the other half, to recall $A-D$ (the second pair shown).

The purpose of these procedures was to see if the memory for order of the $A-B$ and $A-D$ pairs from the 1971 Lists would be poorer than the memory for order of the pairs from the 1968 Lists. Generally speaking, the memory for the correct pair (whether $A-B$ or $A-D$) was somewhat better for the 1968 Lists than for the 1971 Lists, the six subjects tested giving an average of 6.83 and 4.83 correct responses, respectively. If the subject did not respond correctly, it would have resulted from the failure to produce either the $A-B$ or $A-D$ pair, or by giving $A-B$ when $A-D$ was requested, or vice versa. Such instances would indicate a breakdown in the memory for temporal ordering. There were 13 cases of such breakdown for the 1968 Lists and 11 for the 1971 Lists. Even adjusting for differences in number of correct responses, it appeared to us at the time that the technique was not sufficiently encouraging to pursue it.

EXPERIMENT 11

This experiment was designed to study temporal coding of the 1968 and 1971 Lists by use of a within-list design. In the basic condition, the study list consisted of 48 pairs representing all of the $A-B$, $A-D$ pairs from the two sets of lists. In the study lists, the lag between $A-B$ and $A-D$ was systematically varied, there being 3, 6, 9, or 12 other pairs falling between the occurrence of $A-B$ and the occurrence of $A-D$. On the unpaced test, the subjects were given the 24 sets of $A-B$, $A-D$ pairs and were asked to: (1) indicate whether $A-B$ or $A-D$ had occurred most recently in the list; and (2) judge how many other pairs separated the two test pairs in the study list (lag judgments).

As is apparent, the central purpose was to see if we could detect differences in temporal discrimination—either by recency judgments or lag judgments—for the items in the 1968 and 1971 Lists. Given that we could, it would then be possible, perhaps, to turn to studies in which certain of the differences in item characteristics could be examined in a very efficient way. The full description of the experiment (to be given shortly) will show that in addition to pair differentiation we asked also about stimulus-term discrimination and response-term discrimination in independent conditions.

A secondary purpose of the experiment was to inquire into the degree to which a within-list temporal discrimination can be acquired over multiple training and test trials. It was noted in earlier chapters that within-list temporal discriminations are, in any way of viewing the results, very poor after a single inspection trial. With long lists of unrelated words, there is sometimes no evidence that any temporal discriminations were established (e.g., Hintzman, Summers & Block, 1975). In Experiment 2, reported in Chapter 1, lists of 32 unrelated words were used, and there was evidence of some discrimination in both the recency and the lag judgments, but many subjects performed at a chance level. Across the four lists given the subjects in that study, there was no suggestion that the subject learned how to become proficient in making within-list discriminations. Insofar as I have been able to discover, no investigator has previously asked about the course of acquisition of a temporal discrimination over trials when a single list is given multiple trials. How rapidly will subjects become proficient in making lag judgments and in making recency decisions?

Method

In describing the experiment, it will be useful to show the basic study list. This may be seen in Table 3. An inspection of the list will show 24 $A-B$, $A-D$ pairs, 12 from the 1968 Lists and 12 from the 1971 Lists. For each list, three $A-B$, $A-D$ pairs have a lag of 3, three a lag of 6, three a lag of 9, and three have a lag of 12. (In fact, problems in establishing appropriate lags resulted in one $A-B$, $A-D$ lag being 4, rather than 3, and one being 13, rather than 12). Roughly, an $A-B$ and $A-D$ pair at each lag occurs in each third of the list. Two other points about the list construction should be made. First,

TABLE 3
Basic Study List Used in Experiment 11

cot–gloomy	doctor–question	daily–human
kin–rural	bug–double	market–herself
jaw–constant	ham–remote	second–spirit
outside–meeting	children–toward	tug–dirty
elm–haughty	market–island	modern–decide
kin–insane	listen–degree	member–supply
children–river	ham–rotten	mar–lazy
bug–empty	sly–fruitful	gum–speedy
uncle–honor	express–gentle	lid–sturdy
doctor–enjoy	daily–sudden	single–heaven
cot–playful	lid–absurd	tug–barren
elm–angry	wig–tranquil	gum–cheerful
uncle–flower	mar–wicked	member–fellow
outside–army	express–effort	single–suggest
wig–modest	sly–healthy	modern–sugar
jaw–frigid	listen–city	second–golden

Note: The 48 pairs were presented in a single list, not in three groups.

a second form was devised in which the positions of the pairs for the 1968 and 1971 Lists were interchanged, so that across the two forms combined, positions were exactly the same for the two sets of lists. At the same time, in constructing the second form, different $A-B$, $A-D$ pairs were used to represent different lags (as referenced by the first form), so that, across the two forms, six different $A-B$, $A-D$ pairs occurred at each lag. Second, one buffer pair was used at the beginning (*cloudy-urn*), and one pair was used at the end (*sack-misty*).

With the list shown in Table 3 as a reference, we may now describe the five conditions of the experiment.

Condition P—P. The study list (pairs presented: P) was as shown in Table 3, and pairs (P) were tested. Thus, on the test, the subjects were shown 24 pairs of pairs and were asked to circle the most recent pair in each pair of pairs. They were also to circle one number in the series 1 through 16 to indicate the lag. For example:

cot—playful   cot—gloomy   1 2 3 4 5 6 7 8 9 10 11 12 13 14 15 16

The subjects circled the pair they judged to have been most recent in the list and circled a number to indicate the number of other pairs falling between the two test pairs.

Condition P—S. The study list was the same as for Condition P—P but on the test only the 24 stimulus terms (S) were shown, and the subjects made lag judgments. That is, a judgment was made of the number of pairs falling between the two pairs in which the stimulus term appeared.

Condition P—R. The study list was the same as for Condition P—P, but on the test the subject was shown 24 pairs of response terms (R), each pair representing the two words occurring with a common stimulus word in the study list. The subject made a recency judgment and a lag judgment.

Condition S—S. Only the stimulus terms were presented for study (the order being the same as in Table 3 for that form), and on the test the 24 words occurred singly with the subjects required to make lag judgments.

Condition R—R.   Only the 48 response words were presented for study (the order being the same as in Table 3 for that form). On the test, the subject was tested as in Condition P—R.

Under all conditions the items were presented for study at a 4-second rate. The test was unpaced, but the subject was required to make a decision for all items. The order of the test items was random with respect to study order and was subject only to the restriction that each of the four lags be represented once in each successive four test items. When recency judgments were required on the test, the most recent item or pair occurred first half the time and second half the time.

Under all conditions, three study-test cycles were given. The study list and the test list were exactly the same on all three trials. Before the first study trial, the subject was fully informed of the nature of the study list and the nature of the test to be given. After the first test, the subjects were informed that they would be given a second study trial and a test which were exactly the same as the first. This instruction was repeated after the second test trial.

Five independent groups, of 20 subjects each, were used to represent the five conditions. The subjects were assigned to conditions by a block-randomized schedule. All subjects were tested individually, a memory drum being used to present the items on the study trial.

Results

Recency judgments.   The recency judgments given by the subjects in three of the conditions (P—P, P—R, R—R) will be examined initially. First, it may be reported that the number of correct recency judgments did not differ for the 1968 and 1971 Lists, and these lists did not interact with any of the other variables. Therefore, the items from the lists were pooled to examine lag and trial effects. Two plots are shown in Figure 12, the upper one showing the percentage of correct responses as a function of condition and lag, and the lower one showing the percentage of correct responses as a function of trial and lag. An unexpected finding was the lack of influence of lag on the recency judgments. Although there was a small upturn suggested at lag 12, lag as a main effect fell appreciably short of significance

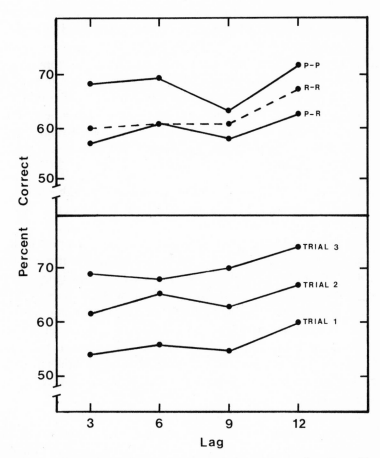

FIGURE 12. Percentage of correct recency judgments as a function of lag and condition (upper panel) and as a function of lag and trials (lower panel) (Experiment 11).

(p = .10), and it did not interact with any other variable. There was a significant effect of conditions, $F(2, 57)$ = 3.62, p = < .05. However, tested independently, neither of the two sets of adjacent conditions differed reliably. The significant effect was largely due to the superiority of Condition P–P over the other two. This indicates that the presence of the stimulus terms facilitated the recency judgments.

The lower plot shows that there was learning across the three trials, but the amount of learning from trial to trial did not differ as a function of lag. No interaction between two variables even approached statistical reliability. Although learning was apparant, the amount should not be exaggerated. Of the 60 subjects in the three conditions combined, 8 scored below chance in terms of total correct responses across three trials, and we may presume that an equal number scored above chance even though they responded randomly. As may be seen in Figure 12, on the first trial, the scores were only slightly above chance (50%).

Lag judgments.   All five conditions required the subject to make lag judgments. In order to establish the proper perspective on these judgments, a plot of the overall results is shown using a scale for the ordinate that is appropriate for the true lags. This plot is shown as Figure 13. Statistically, there was a lag function summing across the 100 subjects (p = .001), but when plotted as in Figure 13, it is almost not discernable. Furthermore, there was no increase in the slope of the lag function. That is, there was no learning across the three trials. The judgments at short lags are a little lower on Trials 2 and 3 as should be expected if learning was occurring, but with long lags, there was no corresponding increase across trials in the lags assigned. In short, in this situation, subjects do not appear capable of learning lag differences.

The next steps were taken to simplify the data somewhat for more detailed presentation. The data showed that lag judgments would not be a satisfactory way to distinguish between possible discriminability differences of the 1968 and 1971 Lists. In none of the conditions was there a difference in the slopes of the lag function for the two sets of lists. We may therefore collapse across this variable for further examination of the data. We may further eliminate Condition R–R and Condition P–R since the lag functions for these two conditions did not approach statistical reliability, whereas in all of the other three conditions the lag slope was highly reliable (p < .01, in each of the three conditions). The distinction between the two sets of conditions is that, in the three conditions in which a lag function was obtained (P–P, S–S, P–S), the judgment could be made on the

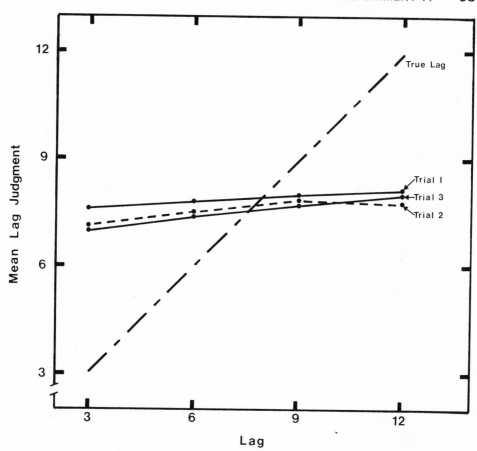

FIGURE 13. Lag judgments for all conditions combined as a function of lag and trials (Experiment 11).

basis of a repeated item (repeated stimulus terms) rather than on the basis of two different items (the response terms in Condition P–R and Condition R–R). This difference confirms previous findings of other invesitgators (e.g., Hintzman, Summers, & Block, 1975). The lag functions for the three conditions showing statistical relia-bility are plotted in Figure 14. Although the mean values may differ from trial to trial, there is at best meager indication that the slopes of the lag functions become consistently and appreciably steeper

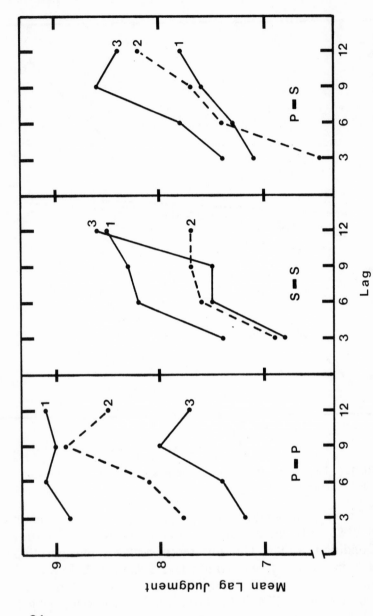

FIGURE 14. Lag judgments as a function of trials (1, 2, 3), lag, and condition (*P–P*, *S–S*, *P–S*) (Experiment 11).

94

across trials. It is not apparent why, in one case (Condition P–P), the values assigned to all lags tend to decrease across trials, and, in another, they tend to increase (Condition P–S).

We had hoped to relate recency judgments and lag judgments in the three conditions in which both responses were required. However, slope measures obtained for individual subjects were completely unreliable. We then examined lag judgments for subjects with many correct recency responses and compared them with the lag judgments for subjects having a low number of correct recency responses. The slopes did not differ in the expected manner. We examined differences in judgments for items occurring in the various sections of the study list and could find no evidence of a serial position curve or any other relationship that was systematic and comparable across conditions. This is to say that none of our internal analyses helped in understanding the results as presented in Figures 12, 13, and 14.

Our search for differences in temporal discriminations for the 1968 and 1971 Lists was not aided by this experiment, but we discovered two facts which we have found surprising. First, a subject will learn within-list recency relationships across trials, but this learning is completely independent of lag and occurs slowly. Second, lag judgments improve very little across trials, and, with unrelated words, true lag had no influence on lag judgments on any trial. These facts must necessarily enter the picture when we attempt to summarize the implications of our work in the last chapter. For the time being, the central chase continues with a further experiment.

EXPERIMENT 12

Earlier I referred to a possible erroneous conclusion drawn from experiments in which $A-B$ had been distributed over several days (Underwood & Ekstrand, 1966). In Experiment 12, the validity of this conclusion was tested. In order to understand the issue, three different conditions must be kept in mind. Assuming that 32 trials will be given on $A-B$, the three conditions may be shown as follows, with the numbers referring to number of learning trials:

	Monday	Tuesday	Wednesday	Thursday	Friday
Distributed	$A-B$, 8	$A-B$, 8	$A-B$, 8	$A-B$, 8: $A-D$	Recall $A-D$
Massed, 3 days	$A-B$, 32	—	—	$A-B$, 32: $A-D$	Recall $A-D$
Massed, 0 days	—	—	—	$A-B$, 32: $A-D$	Recall $A-D$

Because the recall performance under the first two schedules was essentially the same and because both were much higher than recall under the third schedule, it had been concluded that the same mechanism was involved in the reduction in proactive inhibition. That is, some form of temporal discrimination was established when $A-B$ learning was either initiated or completed on Monday, and this differentiation, being much higher than for the third condition, resulted in the large difference in proactive interference between the first two conditions and the third. Of course, these findings held only for the 1968 Lists.

Our subsequent studies have shown that it is not advisable to compare quantitative values across experiments when the experimental history of the subjects is not controlled. The same quantitative outcome by the different procedures may have been quite fortuitous, and the underlying mechanisms may be quite different. Or, it may be that there is some overlap in the mechanisms, but it is incomplete. Finally, it may be that the original decision that both of the first two conditions outlined above bring in the same temporal discrimination was the correct decision. The results for the 1971 Lists showed no effect of the temporal separation between $A-B$ and $A-D$ learning. In Experiment 12, the $A-B$ learning for these lists was spaced over days exactly as indicated in the distributed condition above. The usual zero-interval control was used (the third condition above), in which $A-B$ was learned on Thursday, followed immediately by the learning of $A-D$. If recall does not differ for the two conditions, it will be concluded that the original decision was correct. If a significant slope is found, it will be concluded that the original conclusion was incorrect. Further, given the later outcome and, to some extent, depending upon the magnitude of the slope, a conclusion may be reached that the mechanisms underlying the two phenomena are quite different.

It should be noted that this experiment is not aimed directly at the solution of the puzzle that has occupied our attention. Nevertheless, a positive outcome to the experiment would reduce the scope of the implications of the puzzle.

Method

The method has been out.ined above. The 1971 Lists were used. The 20 subjects in the DP Group were given 32 anticipation trials on $A-B$ at the rate of 8 trials per day for four successive days, Monday through Thursday. Immediately after the 8 $A-B$ trials were administered on Thursday, the $A-D$ list was given, with the criterion of learning being one perfect trial. The 20 subjects in the MP Group were given all 32 trials on $A-B$ on Thursday, followed immediately by $A-D$. Both groups had paced recall of $A-D$ on Friday, 24 hours after learning. All other procedures were the same as in the previous experiments.

Results

The learning of $A-B$ for the two groups of subjects may be compared on the first eight trials. The mean total correct responses were 58.45 for the MP Group, 67.60 for the DP Group. The corresponding mean numbers of trials to learn $A-D$ to one perfect trial were 8.90 and 6.20. Both sets of scores indicate that the performance of the subjects in the DP Groups was better than that for the subjects in the MP Groups. However, neither of the differences was reliable statistically.

The mean number of correct responses on the recall trial was 4.95 (41.3%) for the MP Group, and 5.50 (45.8%) for the DP Group ($F < 1$). The corresponding mean numbers of trials to relearn were 4.10 and 3.85 ($F < 1$). The subjects in the MP Group produced 15 intrusions in recall and relearning of $A-D$; the subjects in the DP Group produced 3.

The results are quite unambiguous. Distributing the $A-B$ learning of the 1971 Lists over four days did not change the conclusions concerning the temporal differentiation of the two interfering lists. Neither the separation of $A-B$ and $A-D$ learning by several days, nor the distribution of $A-B$ learning over several days, produced any influence on the recall of $A-D$ after 24 hours. Both types of operations have produced wide differences in recall of $A-D$ for the 1968 Lists.

SUMMARY

It has been said that even some who participate in the exhilaration of a foxhunt are secretly delighted when the fox eludes the hounds and creeps away to be the object of pursuit another day. I find that mixed emotions attend the end of the present chase. It would not be correct to say that I am delighted that our attempt to solve the case of the missing slope was essentially a failure. At the same time, there is some positive affect attending the following two conclusions:

1. Beyond reasonable doubt, one (or more) of the differences among the characteristics that distinguish the 1968 and 1971 Lists represents a formidable variable in determining temporal coding, hence in determining proactive interference. In one case, memory for the order of the two lists was an integral part of the overall memory for the words in the lists; in the other case, this part of the memory was never evident in the recall performance of the subjects.

2. The attempt to develop short-term procedures to investigate more efficiently the influence of differences in word characteristics for the 1968 and 1971 Lists was not fruitful. Yet, Experiment 11 (which was the major experiment using short-term techniques), produced two surprising (to me) discoveries. First, recency judgments improved across trials, but the improvement was independent of the separation of the two target words (or pairs of target words) in the lists. Second, the subjects were found to be incapable of learni: g (over three trials) the degree to which the target words were separated in the lists. These findings, plus some of those to be reported in the following chapter, have allowed me to repress to some extent the memory of the failures described in this chapter.

5
Beyond the Puzzle

It has been noted that, although our interest in temporal coding was generated by the puzzle, decisions had been made to extend our research beyond that instigated by the case of the missing slope. In Chapter 2, various attributes were discussed as possible vehicles by which temporal coding might be established. One of these, which has figured prominently in theoretical formulations for various phenomena, is context. Simply stated, different contexts may become associated with different target memories and these contexts may be more easily remembered than the targets. But, to repeat what was said in Chapter 2, there seems to be no easy way to get context memories to mediate temporal discriminations, unless the contexts have calendarlike properties or are associated with memories with such properties. It does not seem that contexts, no matter how memorable, can produce temporal ordering simply because they are remembered better. Still, as has been seen, some experiments turn very unexpected findings, so the issue should not be severely pre-judged.

Three experiments will be reported on context effects and their role in temporal discriminations. The first two involve between-list manipulations, while the third involves a within-list approach. A fourth study looked at temporal coding as a function of the number of different events falling between target items and at the relationships among temporal coding, frequency assimilation, and associative learning.

EXPERIMENT 13

It has sometimes been suggested that "internal" context represents the most effective type of context manipulation when dealing with relatively short temporal intervals. This internal context might include covert thoughts, moods, or emotions of the subject which occur at the time the task is given. In Experiment 13, an examination was made of the influence of a somewhat different type of internal context. For lack of a better term, I will call this *process context* or *mechanism context*. The approach carries the assumption that the learning of different verbal tasks requires (to some degree, at least) different processes or mechanisms. Insofar as these processes differ, they will produce a different internal context for the words occurring in the different tasks.

There is some evidence in the literature that could be interpreted to mean that process context can serve to differentiate two lists. For example, Shuell and Keppel (1967) asked about retroactive inhibition when the two lists were learned as serial tasks, when both were learned as free-recall tasks, or when one was learned as a serial task and the other as a free-recall task. In short, the independent variable was the same or different type of tasks. These investigators found that retroactive inhibition was less under the different conditions than under the same conditions. They point out that the interpretation of the finding is not without ambiguity. It may be that the different tasks produced better temporal differentiation under the different condition than under the same condition, or the results could be interpreted to be a consequence of differences in unlearning. Nevertheless, the results of this experiment are suggestive of the potential of process context as a means of producing temporal differentiation.

In the present experiment, the subjects learned four successive lists, following which they were asked to indicate the list membership for each word in all of the lists. In the different condition (Condition D), the four lists were constituted as four different tasks: a verbal-discrimination list (VD), a paired-associate list (PA), a serial list (SR), and a free-recall list (FR). In the same condition (Condition S), all four lists were of the same class. If process context differences aid temporal coding, list identification should be superior for the subjects given Condition D than for those given Condition S. Two features of the experiment should be emphasized. First, we went to some extreme to be sure that the list numbers (1, 2, 3, 4) occurred several times during the learning of a list. The purpose of this was, of course, to establish opportunity for associations to develop among contexts, items, and a simple ordering system. Second, we gave three acquisition trials on all lists in order that it would become highly improbable that a subject would fail to recognize a word at the time of the list-identification test.

Method

Lists.　　Each of the four lists was made up of 16 words. The 64 words constituted a random sample of a larger random sample of two-syllable words with frequencies of from 1 to 10 in the Thorndike-Lorge tables (1944). The 64 words were assigned randomly to one of four lists of 16 words each, and the numbers 1 through 4 assigned to the lists. For all conditions of the experiment, the order of the lists was 1 through 4, as indicated by the above assignment. For each set of 16 words, the four types of lists were constructed. These consisted of 8 pairs of words for PA and VD and 16 single items for FR and SR.

Conditions.　　There were six conditions, four representing S conditions and two representing D conditions, with 20 subjects in each of the six groups assigned to conditions by a block-randomized schedule. The four S conditions may be identified as VD–S, PA–S, SR–S, and FR–S. In these conditions, a given group learned four successive lists of the same type. There were two D conditions, which will be identified as D1 and D2. In Condition D1, a subject learned four different types of lists. By varying the order of the lists within subgroups, each list type occurred equally often (five times) at each of the four positions, when viewed across all subjects. Furthermore, in no case did a VD list and a PA list occupy adjacent positions within the series of four positions. Likewise, FR and SR lists never occupied adjacent positions. It seemed possible to us that the lists might be distinguished on the basis of pair presentation versus single-item presentation on the study trials. In Condition D1, therefore, this confounding of adjacency of list position and context similarity was avoided. In Condition D2, this confounding was present. The order of the lists was arranged so that the SR and FR lists were always adjacent (Positions 1 and 2 or Positions 3 and 4), and the same was true for the PA and VD lists. As can be seen, however, it was still possible to maintain the rule that, across the 20 subjects, each list type occurred equally often (five times) at each of the four positions in the series.

Procedure.   There were three study-test cycles for each list. On the study trials, the rate of presentation on the memory drum was 4 seconds per pair (VD and PA) or two seconds per item (FR and SR). The test for learning, given after each trial, was limited to one minute, during which the subject wrote his responses. For tests on the SR lists, each recall sheet contained 16 numbered blanks, and the subject was asked to write the words in the correct position. For tests on the FR lists, the subject wrote his responses on a sheet with 16 unnumbered blanks. For PA, the 8 stimulus terms were presented with a blank after each, and the subject was asked to write in the appropriate response terms. For the VD tests, the 8 pairs were shown, and the subject was required to circle the member of the pair that had been underlined (correct word) on the study trial. The order of the items or pairs differed for each study trial for the VD, PA, and FR lists, but, of course, the order was always the same for the SR lists. A single order of the pairs was used for the three test trials for the PA and VD tasks.

In the initial instructions, the subjects were informed that they would be given three study-test trials on each of four lists. The nature of the tests for learning were also described. The experimentalist always referred to each list by the appropriate number, and the list number was mentioned before each study trial. Furthermore, the list number appeared on the memory drum tape before each study trial and on each test sheet for each trial. At the minimum, therefore, each list number was given nine times, three times by the experimenter and six times by the notations on the tape and test sheets.

For the D conditions, it was necessary for the experimenter to give new instructions for each successive task. We abbreviated these instructions as much as possible. To keep the interlist interval about the same for the S conditions as for the D conditions, the experimenter simply repeated the original instructions for the particular type of task after the completion of the learning for each list in the S conditions.

After the third trial on the fourth list, each subject was given five minutes to work on the pyramid puzzle. Following this interval, the instructions for the list identification task were read. At no time before this point had the subject been informed that such a test would be given. The test was paced at a 5-second rate, and the subjects were forced to respond to each word with a number (1, 2, 3, or 4), to indicate the list membership of each of the 64 words. The order of the items on the test was randomized, subject to the restriction that one word from each of the four lists be represented in each successive block of four words.

Results

Learning.   As a measure of learning, the mean total number of correct responses for three trials was used. For Conditions S–PA and S–SR, performance from the first to the second list improved somewhat (learning-to-learn) and then remained roughly constant for the three lists beyond the first. For Condition S–FR, the learning was roughly constant across all four lists, and this was also true for Condition S–VD. Indeed, performance on the VD lists was essentially perfect on all trials. Of the 20 subjects in Condition S–VD, 13 failed to make an error across the 12 trials. Summing across the four lists, the mean total correct responses per list were 23.74, 18.66, 21.58, and 26.00 for VD, PA, SR, and FR, respectively, with a maximum of 24 possible for VD and PA, and 48 possible for SR and FR. After combining Conditions D1 and D2, the mean correct responses per list corresponding to those for the S conditions were found to be 23.58, 18.40, 19.78, and 28.38. Essentially, then, the levels of learning achieved under Conditions D and S were the same for lists of a given type.

List identification.   The mean numbers of errors made on each of the four lists for the six conditions are shown in Figure 15. For each list, the maximum possible number of errors was 16, and sheer guessing should have produced a mean of 12 errors. The results for the four S conditions are in the left panel of the figure, those for the two D conditions in the right panel. It may first be noted that summed across the four lists, there were fewer errors under the two

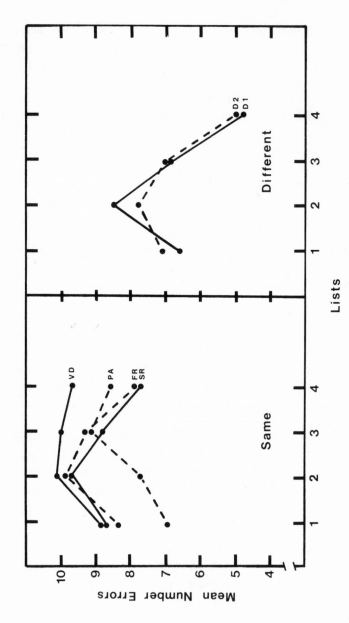

FIGURE 15. List-identification errors on the four lists as a function of learning the same type of lists or different types of lists (Experiment 13).

104

D conditions than under the four S conditions, the means per list being 8.84 and 6.71, respectively (t = 3.96). This finding indicates that what I have called process context facilitated temporal discrimination.

Looking at the left panel, it can be seen that there were differences in correct identification as a function of type of task, $F(3, 78)$ = 3.44, $p < .05$. The effect is primarily to be attributed to the relatively good performance under Condition S–PA on the first two lists and poor performance under Condition S–VD on lists 3 and 4. The number of errors was also influenced by the position of the list in the series of four lists, $F(3, 228) = 4.53, p < .01$. Generally speaking, there were primacy and recency effects for lists, but these were not neat and clean for all list types. Although the figure suggests an interaction between type of task and list, statistically, this interaction fell short of an acceptable level of significance ($F = 1.40$). The mean total errors across the four lists were 32.40, 38.55, 35.00, and 35.40 for PA, VD, SR, and FR, respectively. Two subjects, both in Condition S–VD, scored worse than chance (48.00).

As seen in the right panel of Figure 15, performance on the first two lists for the D conditions was about at the same level as was that on the first two lists for Condition S–PA. The most noticeable influence of the context differences occurs on the last two lists. In recording the data from the D conditions, it became quite apparent that many of the subjects had error scores that were well within the range of scores for the S conditions. A distribution of the 40 scores showed evidence of bimodality. The 40 subjects were divided at the median and the means for each subgroup determined; these values were 15.80 and 36.00 total errors. The latter value approximates the mean of the 80 subjects in the S condition (35.34). As would be expected in view of the above facts, the standard deviations differed for the subjects in the S and D conditions, being 6.30 for the 80 subjects in the S condition and 12.67 for the 40 subjects in the D conditions. To describe these results in sharpest terms: About half the subjects in the D groups were markedly influenced by the context manipulation; about half were not influenced at all.

We may ask about list-identification errors as a function of type of list for the two D conditions combined. There were 40 subjects for each type of list, and since list type was counterbalanced, it is permissable to look at the four means representing list types, each being based on 40 subjects. The means were 6.15, 7.10, 6.68, and 7.05 for PA, VD, SR, and FR, respectively ($F < 1$). Thus, the facilitation produced by context was about the same for all types of lists.

The next step is to ask about error sources. When an error was made on a given word, with what list was it identified? The manipulations in this experiment involved three kinds of similarity, each of which could be a potential source of confusion. There is first the similarity produced by the differences in temporal closeness of the lists; adjacent lists are more similar (closer together) than are non-adjacent lists. Lists 1 and 4 represent the extreme (least close). Second, the manipulation of process context in Condition D1 was aimed at reducing the deleterious effect of temporal closeness on list identification. Third, with respect to Condition D2, insofar as pair presentation versus single-item presentation in the lists can serve as a discriminative cue, error sources should be influenced. The pair-single variable might influence performance either because of the superficial perceptual differences or because there is a concomitant process difference, or both. We have already seen that the total number of errors did not differ for Conditions D1 and D2. It remains to be seen whether error sources differ under the two conditions.

When errors on each list were plotted as a function of the list identified in the error, the plots closely resembled temporal generalization gradients. The closeness of lists was clearly seen to be a determinant of error frequency. These gradients do not, however, provide the best means of depicting the differences in error sources for the various conditions of the experiment. An alternative method is shown in Table 4. These data show the percent of total errors produced by an interchange of errors between all combinations of two lists. The values for the four S conditions differed very little and were therefore combined in Table 4. The percentages for Conditions D1 and D2 are shown separately.

A comparison of D1 and D2 shows that adjacent lists constructed of pairs (Lists 1 and 2 or Lists 3 and 4) and adjacent lists in which single items were presented produced two consequences. First, the errors increased between the two adjacent lists, and, second, the errors between the first two lists and the last two lists decreased. The first result is given by a comparison of Lists 1 and 2, and Lists 3 and 4 across the two conditions. A comparison of the two conditions on all of the remaining combinations gives the support for the second conclusion. These effects are precisely what should occur if the pair-single manipulation was a relevant context manipulation. To produce these effects, of course, required that temporal closeness be involved. In effect, the similarities between the PA and VD lists and the SR and FR lists increased the influence of the temporal closeness.

There is at best only suggestive evidence that the pair-single variable had an influence when not supported by the highest level of temporal closeness (adjacency). In Condition D1, the pair-single variable should, if effective, have increased the interchange of errors between Lists 1 and 3 and Lists 2 and 4. Comparing the percents for Condition D1 with those for the S conditions shows that the errors are greater for Lists 1 and 3 for Condition D1 than for the S conditions, but this is not true for Lists 2 and 4. It must be emphasized that the error scores in Table 4 are reciprocal within a condition. If one category has an increase (relative to that category in another condition), some one or more other categories must show a decrease. We might presume that the relatively high value for Lists 1 and 3 in Condition D1 results from the pair-single variable, but since most of the decrease occurs for Lists 3 and 4 (as opposed to

TABLE 4
Percentage of Errors between Pairs of Lists (Experiment 13)

List combinations	Conditions		
	D1	D2	S
1 & 2	24.3	31.7	20.7
1 & 3	20.2	19.3	13.7
1 & 4	4.5	4.3	5.6
2 & 3	26.2	13.9	27.7
2 & 4	10.7	7.2	10.9
3 & 4	14.0	23.6	21.5

being spread over all combinations), we cannot be sure just what is responsible. Nevertheless, we can be sure that the comparisons for Conditions D1 and D2 show that the pair-single variable had an influence on error sources.

Learning and temporal discrimination: S conditions.   We will now examine the tasks used in the S conditions to seek relationships between performance in learning and performance on the list-identification test. Each task will be examined in turn, starting with the PA lists.

There was a relationship between the total correct responses in PA learning and errors in list identification when viewed by subjects. The correlation for the 20 subjects was −.46 ($p < .05$). It might be expected that the act of responding (writing) a word during the study-test cycles would lead to better list identification than not responding. The only "clean" test for this was to ask about differences in the identification of stimulus terms versus response terms. The mean number of errors on the stimulus terms was 16.30 and on the response terms, 16.10. As a second way of looking at this matter, we asked if there was a correlation between the number of errors made on stimulus terms and the number made on the paired response terms. This correlation for the 32 pairs was .25, a value which is not significantly different from zero. Thus there are three conclusions regarding list-identification errors for Condition S−PA. First, subjects who are the better learners tend to make fewer errors than those who are the poorer learners; second, association of items with lists is not dependent upon responding in learning; and, third, the basis for errors made to the stimulus term and to the response term in a pair is different. We have not discovered any reasonable explanation of why the performance on the first two lists under Condition S−PA was better than the performance on those lists under the other three S conditions.

The learning of the lists under Condition S−VD was so high that little variability existed. Therefore, a correlation between total correct responses and list-identification errors across subjects or items would have little meaning. However, we may ask whether the errors differed for the underlined (correct) words and for the nonunderlined (incorrect words). The average number of errors made on the correct words by the 20 subjects was 17.75 and, on the incorrect words, 20.80. The difference was reliable ($t = 3.08$). There is reason to believe that, in learning a VD list, the experienced subject will develop a strategy of attending only to the underlined word on the study trials. If this occurred in the present study, the subject may not even have recognized a word on the test trials that had not been underlined on the study trials. If the strategy of ignoring these words develops with experience in learning VD lists, it would be anticipated that the difference in list-identification errors for correct and incorrect words should increase across the four lists. This, in fact, occurred. On the first two lists, a total of 189 errors was made to the underlined or correct words, 190 to the nonunderlined or incorrect words. The corresponding values for the third and fourth lists combined were 167 and 225. This difference probably accounts for the fact that the overall number of errors on the VD lists (as seen in Figure 15) remains high on the third and fourth lists. The decrease in the number of errors for the correct words on these two lists (relative to the first two) is less than the increase in the number of errors for the incorrect words. Had we required the subjects to pronounce both words on the VD study trials, it seems very likely that the results for the VD lists would have been much the same as for the FR and SR lists.

Turning next to Condition S–FR, we first correlated the total correct responses given in learning the four lists by the 20 subjects and the number of errors made on the list-identification test. This correlation was only $-.12$. We then determined the number of times that each of the 64 words was given correctly (summing across subjects) during learning and correlated these values with the number of list-identification errors for each word. This value was $-.24$, which is of borderline reliability. Thus again, it appears that the association of words with list numbers is not influenced appreciably by responding with the words during learning.

Finally the results for Condition S–SR (serial lists) will be examined. The total correct responses given in learning the four lists for each subject was correlated with the number of list-identification errors. This correlation was $-.15$. As a next step, serial-position curves were determined by summing across subjects and lists to obtain the number of correct responses given at each serial position.

These values were then transformed to percentages based on the total correct responses across all positions. Then, the number of errors in list identification made on words at each serial position was determined, again summing across subjects and lists, and these values were transformed to percent errors at each position based on total errors at all positions. The relationship between these two sets of values is shown in Figure 16. It is very evident that the usual bowed, skewed curve for correct responding was found for these lists. It is equally clear that errors in list identification have little to do with correct responding during learning.

Taken as a whole, the results of the above analyses for the S conditions are remarkable for the *lack* of relationships between

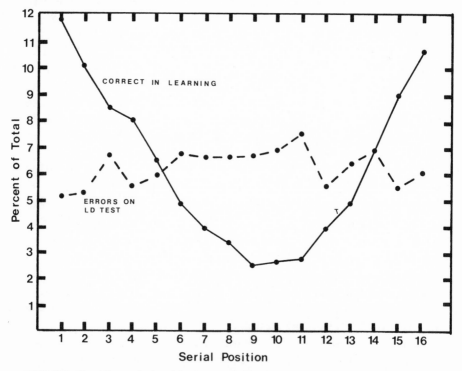

FIGURE 16. The relationship between the number of correct responses at each position of a serial list and the number of list-identification errors made for the words at each position (Experiment 16).

learning measures and list-identification errors, whether viewed by subjects or by items. Learning ability and ability in making temporal judgments were moderately related for the PA lists, but this relationship was not evident for either the SR or FR lists. The number of times an item was correctly recalled in learning was not related to its likelihood of being correctly identified with its list on the temporal test.

Learning and Temporal discrimination: D conditions.   When the 40 subjects in the two D conditions were divided at the median of the distribution of error scores, 10 subjects from each condition fell in the high-error group, and 10 fell in the low-error group. In pursuit of other evidence, which might distinguish between these two subgroups who differed so markedly as a function of process context, we have made a number of analyses involving learning measures using these two subgroups of 20 subjects. At the same time, we made other analyses that involved all 40 subjects. The results of some of these analyses will be described briefly as a series of points.

1. The correlation between total correct responses in learning the four lists and number of errors made on the temporal test was $-.37$ for the 40 subjects. Although this correlation would be judged statistically reliable ($p < .05$), the amount of shared variance is obviously quite low. The correlations were calculated between learning scores on each task (excepting VD) and list-identification errors. All were negative, but only one, that for SR, was reliable ($r = -.43$).

2. If the processes or mechanisms underlying the learning of the four tasks are different (as assumed by the notion of process context), the correlations for number of correct responses in learning the various tasks should be low. Of the three possible correlations (again, the VD task was not included), only the one between PA and FR was reliably different from zero ($r = .45$), suggesting that these two tasks have more in common than do the other combinations. The errors made in list identification for Condition D1 give little support for this commonality. In identifying items from PA lists, the distribution of errors was 39.6%, 24.3%, and 36.0% from FR, VD, and SR lists, respectively. For errors made in identifying

items from FR lists, the values were 32.4%, 35.3%, and 32.4%, from the PA, VD, and SR lists, respectively.

The correlations between learning scores for the three tasks were also calculated separately for the two subgroups, which had produced many and few errors in list identification. Both groups showed positive correlations between PA and FR learning (.38 and .27), but the only substantial correlation was a negative relationship between learning the PA and SR lists (−.57) for the subgroup that made few list-identification errors. When this correlation was first calculated, it seemed obvious that an error in calculation had occurred. Recalculations and a scatter plot showed otherwise. The corresponding correlation for the high-error group was .04. It appeared that something unusual had happened and that it should not be swept under the rug.

A negative correlation between learning the PA and SR lists for the subjects making few errors on temporal coding may be interpreted in a number of ways. The most direct and least theoretical interpretation is merely to say that, among these subjects, the possession of superior skills for performance on one task is accompanied by possession of inferior skills for the performance on the other. Since performance on either task did not deviate appreciably from the performance of other subjects, it does not mean that the subjects as a group were good performers on one task and poor performers on the other. Rather, roughly speaking, half were good performers on PA learning and poor performers on SR learning; for the other half, this was reversed. It may be noted that the order in which the PA and SR lists were learned was of no consequence. Indeed, because of some learning-to-learn from PA to SR, and from SR to PA, the true correlation is somewhat underestimated when all 20 subjects were used to estimate the correlation. Looking only at the subjects who had the PA list before the SR list, the correlation was −.65; for those who had the SR list before the PA list the value was −.70.

A strong negative correlation could imply high discriminability between the words in the two lists. Or, such a correlation might imply a positive affect for one list and a negative affect for the other. Or, it might imply antagonistic processes or strategies for the two lists. If discriminability is enhanced, error interchange between the two types of lists (SR and PA) on the list-identification test should be minimal. With some trepidation, I will report that this expectation is given strong support by the data. When an error in list identification was made on a word from a PA list, in only 8.8% of the cases was it assigned the number of the SR list. When an error was made on a word from an SR list, in only 14.1% of the cases was it assigned the number of the PA list. The corresponding values for the high-error subgroup were 24.7% and 31.6%. The two values for the low-error group were the two smallest values in the table of 24 values showing error sources for all types of lists for the high- and low-error groups.

I simply do not understand why subjects who make few errors on list identification for all types of lists showed a negative correlation between PA and SR learning. In addition to being quite unenlightened with regard to the negative correlation, I am not confident that an expectation of fewer interchange of errors for the lists is proper. Nor am I sure that the results could be replicated. Still, perhaps the finding represents a lead that will eventually take someone to Stockholm. It cannot be followed further in this book.

3. The two subgroups showed the same relative number of list-identification errors on all four types of lists. The interaction between subgroups and errors on the four types of lists was less than unity. Good subjects were good on all list types; poor subjects were poor on all list types.

4. Plots for the 40 subjects showing errors as a function of position in the serial lists matched the results for the S conditions as shown in Figure 16.

5. Performance on the underlined (correct) and nonunderlined (incorrect) words in the VD list did not differ for either subgroup of subjects. This supports the idea that a subject must learn several successive VD lists before he will start ignoring the nonunderlined words.

6. Neither subgroup differed on the number of errors made to stimulus terms and to response terms from the PA lists.

7. Performance on each of the four successive quarters of the test list was examined separately for the two subgroups. The subgroup with few total errors showed a reduction in errors from

quarter to quarter for words from all four lists. The subgroup with many total errors showed a small decrease in number of errors from the first to the second quarter, followed by successive increases for the third and fourth quarters. This interaction between subgroups and quarters was reliable, $F(3, 114) = 3.35, p < .05$. It was as if the subjects in the subgroup making few total errors were learning something as they were being tested. The increasing differences between the two subgroups from quarter to quarter should not be overblown; the two groups differed widely even on the first quarter.

Summary

The results of this experiment indicated that process context differences can serve to establish differentiating temporal codes for memories formed at different points in time. The ability to distinguish the temporal order of items in the four lists was markedly enhanced by process context for about half the subjects and was relatively impotent for the other half. This bifurcation may suggest that the information available to the subgroups of subjects might not have differed greatly but that there were differences in the utilization of the information. However, this experiment was not analytical with regard to this issue. The differences between the two subgroups may mean that the associative processes differed and that the test did extract most of the information available to the subjects concerning the list membership of the words.

Another finding to be kept in mind is that the relationships between measures of learning and measures of list identification were, at best, weak. We will have an opportunity to look at this matter in subsequent experiments and thereby obtain some idea of the generality of the finding. It is to be hoped that when all of the experiments are evaluated in the final chapter, some general principles may be educed. We are going to turn immediately to Experiment 14, in which the between-list context manipulation differs from that of Experiment 13.

EXPERIMENT 14

This experiment was designed with three purposes in mind, purposes that may best be understood by describing the tasks given the subjects. All subjects were given eight successive short free-recall lists. After all eight lists had been given, the subjects were given words from each list and were asked (unexpectedly) to identify the list (1 through 8) in which the words had appeared.

The first purpose was to determine if a distinct semantic context for each list would influence list identification. These semantic contexts were induced by having all of the words in a list members of a single category, with eight different categories represented by the eight lists. Each list was given two study trials and one test trial. The assumption was that the category names would be elicited implicitly many times in the act of learning and recalling each list. Therefore, the memory for the category name should be far more memorable than the memories for individual words. The memory for the ordering of the eight category names (if present) should mediate the ordering of the specific words. To eliminate the concept name as a potential ordering code in other conditions, instances of each concept occurred in all eight lists.

The second purpose of the experiment was to determine if external tasks that were different from each other and distinctly different from the free-recall task could serve as effective temporal coding contexts for the words in the free-recall lists. Thus, in some conditions, eight different tasks were given to the subjects, one after each of the eight free-recall lists. These tasks will be described later. In control conditions, the same external task was given after each of the free-recall lists.

The third purpose of the study was to determine if the two types of contexts (semantic and external) would summate or interact in any way in their influence on temporal coding. To this end, conditions were included in which no external tasks were administered between the successive free-recall lists.

In summary, there were three variations of the external context, same (S), different (D), and none (N). Under each of these three contexts, there were two semantic context conditions: one in which all of the words in a list were instances of the same context, or unmixed (U); and one in which instances of each context occurred in each list (mixed or M). The six conditions may be identified by two letters, the first representing the semantic context, the second representing the external context: UN, US, UD, MN, MS, MD. If both context manipulations are effective, maximal list-identification performance should occur under Condition UD, minimal perform-ance under Condition MN.

Method

Lists.   Eight categories were chosen from the Battig-Montague (1969) norms, and, for each category, 11 of the most frequently given words were selected. The eight categories were: alcoholic beverage, weapon, sport, fruit, metal, four-footed animal, kind of cloth, and occupation or profession. Eight of the 11 words in each category were chosen randomly to form the eight lists to be learned as unmixed (U) lists. A single random order of the eight lists was used for all subjects in the learning phase, the order being as listed above. The three words not used in the lists were used as new words on a recognition test given at the end of the session. From among the eight words in each list, three were chosen randomly and used as test words on the list-identification test. Three additional words were selected randomly and used as old words on the recognition test.

The mixed (M) lists were formed of eight words, with one word from each category appearing in each list. These were the same 64 words that were used in the unmixed lists. The mixed lists were constructed so that the 24 list-identification words (three from each list) were exactly the same 24 words as tested from the unmixed lists. The same requirement was imposed for the three words from each list used on the recognition test.

External context tasks.   The eight tasks used in the external context manipulations will be described briefly. The order in which they are described represents the order in which they were given to all subjects in the different (D) conditions.

1. Symbol cancellation. Ten different nonletter typewriter characters or symbols were randomized in horizontal lines of 30 symbols each. In front of each line, three of the symbols were given as those to be crossed out in that line. The three target symbols differed from line to line.

2. Anagrams. The 20 scrambled words all consisted of names of countries, and the subject was informed of this.

3. Arithmetic. Simple addition of sets of eight, two-place numbers.

4. Stroop test. A version consisting of five different color names printed in inappropriate colors of ink.

5. Search Task 1. This task was patterned after the one described by Kappauf and Payne (1959). Pairs of two-digit numbers (e.g., 39-64 were printed in a long column. The experimenter gave the subject a two-digit starting number to be found among the numbers to the left of the hyphen. When the subject found this, the number to the right of the hyphen designated the next target number to be found among the numbers to the left of the hyphens, and so on.

6. Alphabet printing. The subject printed the letters of the alphabet upside down, moving from the right to left on the page.

7. Mirror star tracing. The five-pointed star was a double image with a border six millimeters wide around the edge. The subjects viewed the star in a mirror and, starting at the lower right-hand point, moved their pencils in the border, going counterclockwise.

8. Search Task 2. The numbers 2 through 75 were randomly positioned on a sheet of paper, with the number 1 in the center of the sheet. The subject circled the numbers in order.

As noted earlier, all eight tasks were used when the external context was different for each list. For the same context conditions, a subject had the same task after each of the eight lists. Three tasks were chosen from among the eight (symbol cancellation, Stroop, mirror tracing) to be used for these S conditions. An equal number of subjects was assigned to each.

Procedure.   The subjects were informed initially that they would be given several short free-recall lists to learn. Those subjects assigned to conditions involving external-context tasks were further told that they would be given other tasks for the purpose of discovering how well people can do different kinds of tasks. Each eight-word list was presented for two study trials at a 2-second rate, with a different order of the words on each trial. Following the second study trial, a 30-second recall trial was administered, during which subjects were told to write the words in any order they chose. If an external-context task was called for, 30 seconds were allotted for instructions, followed by a 60-second test on the task. Although the instruction time may have varied somewhat, the 60-second performance test was exactly timed. Immediately after the test on the external-context task, the next free-recall list was given for two study trials, and so on through the eight lists.

In the two conditions where the external context was not given (Conditions UN and MN), a problem of method arose. Ideally, 90 seconds should elapse between each list to correspond to the time required to administer the external-context tasks. What activity should the subject be given during the 90-second interval? A pure blank interval might have led to rehearsal of the lists. Filling the interval with some innocuous task was precisely what was done in the S conditions. The decision was made to omit the 90-second interval. Thus, after the recall of a list, the experimenter immediately gave the study trials on the next list. The consequence is that the lists were more temporally bunched under the two N conditions (MN and UN) than under the other four conditions (US, MS, UD, MD) in which external-context tasks were used.

Following the eighth external task (or following the recall of the eighth list for the N conditions), the list-identification test was given. This was an unpaced test. There were 24 words on the test, three from each list. The subjects were required to assign a number (1 through 8) to indicate their judgment concerning the list membership for each word. The subjects were told that all words had been in the lists, but were not told that the test included three from each list. After this test, the recognition test was described to the subjects. They were told that some of the words had occurred in the eight lists, and that some had not (were new words). The 24 words from the lists and the 24 new words produced a 48-item test, and the subjects were required to make a YES–NO decision for each word. As described earlier, the list-identification test and the recognition test were identical for all six conditions.

One particular aspect of the procedures of this experiment should be emphasized. In contrast to the method used for Experiment 13, list numbers were never used to identify the lists. If a calendarlike ordering device was to develop, it had to be supplied by the subject. Since the subjects did not know that a list-identification test was to be given, there is no reason to believe that they would deliberately set about to devise an ordering system.

Subjects.   A block-randomized schedule was used to assign 24 college students to each of the six conditions. For the two conditions in which the same external task was used throughout (Conditions US and MS), eight subjects were assigned to each of the three tasks.

Results

Learning.   It would be expected that the recall of the words from the unmixed lists would be higher than the recall from the mixed lists. No clear expectations had been developed concerning a possible role for the external context tasks on the free-recall learning. The total correct responses across the eight lists was determined, and these are plotted in terms of percentage of correct of total possible in Figure 17. As can be seen, performance was better on the mixed lists than on the unmixed ($F = 38.45$). The external tasks had no influence on the unmixed lists, but a clear negative influence was evident in the recall of the mixed lists when no intervening task was given between lists (Condition MN). Under Condition MN, performance remained about constant across the eight lists, whereas in all other conditions, performance increased across the lists. The interaction between the two variables was reliable $F(2, 138) = 4.66$, $p < .05$.

Performance on the recognition task (given after the list-identification test) was also better for subjects given the unmixed lists than for those given the mixed lists. Neither the misses nor false alarms differed for either type of list as a function of the external-context manipulation. The number of false alarms (4.2%) was identical for the mixed and unmixed lists. The misses for the 72 subjects given

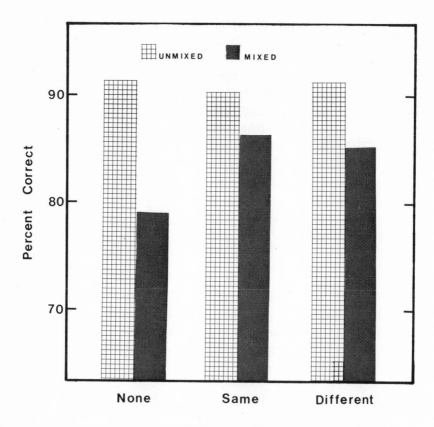

FIGURE 17. Learning of the eight mixed and eight unmixed lists as a function of the external context (Experiment 14).

the unmixed lists averaged 4.0%; for those given the mixed lists, the corresponding value was 9.1% ($F = 22.79$). Roughly speaking, the subjects in the former group failed to recognize just one of the 24 old words, while the subjects in the latter group failed to recognize two old words. It should be noted that the deficit present in recall under Condition MN was not present on the recognition test.

List identification.   On the list-identification test, the 24 words (three from each list) were scrambled, and the subject was required to circle a number to indicate the list membership of each word. The initial response measure used was errors, there being a maximum of three for each list under each condition. The complete data are shown in Table 5. The first step is to reduce these data to a more manageable level. An examination of the last column shows that the external context tasks had no influence on list identification for either the mixed or unmixed lists ($F < 1$). Therefore, this variable may be dismissed from further consideration. In doing so, however, it should be noted that, although the recall of the subjects under Condition MN was less than for the other conditions, list-identification performance was equivalent to that for the other two conditions involving mixed lists.

The mean values for mixed and unmixed lists show that, across all eight lists, performance was better for the unmixed lists. For the first and last unmixed lists, list-identification was essentially perfect. On the other hand, with the mixed lists, the subjects committed about 50% errors on the first and last lists. For the lists in the middle of the series, performance was only slightly better than chance for the subjects having learned the mixed lists.

We had anticipated that list identification for the unmixed lists would reflect all-or-none decisions by the subjects for the three

TABLE 5

Mean Number of List Identification Errors (Three Possible)
as a Function of List Number and Conditions
(Experiment 14)

Condition		1	2	3	4	5	6	7	8	Mean
UN		.17	1.13	2.08	2.21	1.75	2.13	1.29	.04	1.35
US		.25	1.21	1.75	2.08	1.92	1.88	1.63	.13	1.36
UD		.13	.46	1.83	2.13	2.17	2.17	1.08	.13	1.26
	Mean:	.18	.93	1.89	2.14	1.95	2.06	1.33	.10	1.32
MN		1.54	2.33	2.21	2.38	2.29	2.25	2.25	1.21	2.06
MS		1.38	2.42	2.71	2.33	2.42	2.21	2.33	1.33	2.14
MD		1.50	2.13	2.33	2.38	2.38	2.50	2.04	1.33	2.07
	Mean:	1.47	2.29	2.42	2.36	2.36	2.32	2.21	1.29	2.09

words within a concept. That is, the three instances of a concept would all be assigned to the same list; hence, all would be correct or all would be incorrect. Of the 72 subjects who learned the unmixed lists, 78% showed this pattern exactly. The assignments by the remaining subjects suggested that they intended to follow this pattern but simply made a few careless errors in carrying it out.

One problem we had not fully anticipated was produced by the behavior of the subjects given the mixed lists. These subjects assigned more words to the lists in the middle of the series of eight than to the lists on the ends. It was as if they assigned middle-list numbers when in doubt. For reasons that are not clear to me, this tendency differed somewhat for the subjects in the three mixed-list conditions. The central-tendency effect was most exaggerated in Condition MN: There the mean numbers of words assigned to the eight lists were, in order, 2.46, 2.38, 3.33, 4.08, 3.83, 3.63, 2.42, and 1.88. The tendency was minimal in Condition MD, where the values were 2.83, 2.75, 2.96, 3.38, 3.13, 3.46, 3.17, and 2.33.

Various scoring procedures were used to make adjustments for the different number of assignments made to the lists. In fact, no substantial changes resulted from these adjustments. The only clear effect was to increase by a small amount the number of errors for the lists in the middle, but this increase did not result in any clear differences in performance for the three mixed-list conditions. No conclusion was changed. Therefore, I will use the error scores as given in Table 5 to examine in somewhat more detail the differences between the performance on the mixed and unmixed lists. In Figure 18, the error scores for the three mixed lists combined and for the three unmixed lists combined have been plotted to provide a visual picture of the influence of the semantic context. The values are given in terms of percent errors.

It seems beyond doubt that for the unmixed lists "first list" was associated with alcoholic beverages and "last list" with occupations. Some subjects also had knowledge of the concepts involved in the second and seventh list, but beyond this temporal coding was minimal. If the subject had knowledge of the list numbers associated with three or four of the concept names, performance on the remaining lists would not be judged to be a great deal better than chance. In

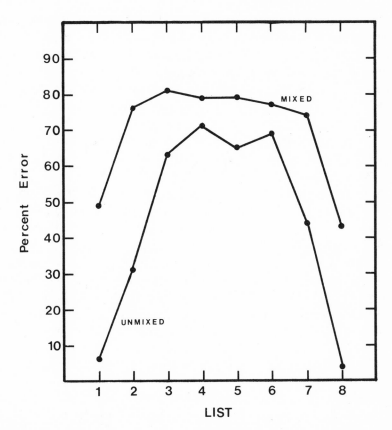

FIGURE 18. Percentage of errors on list identification as related to mixed versus unmixed lists, and as a function of list position (Experiment 14).

fact, it seems reasonable to assume that the differences between the mixed and unmixed lists for the middle four lists may be due to differences associated with guessing. Given that temporal coding for the end lists differs for the mixed and unmixed lists, differential probabilities of correct guessing automatically follow. Semantic context influenced temporal coding for the initial and final lists, but beyond this its influence was of little consequence.

It might be argued that the subjects having unmixed lists had an advantage over the subjects having the mixed lists. With unmixed lists, the subject knew that a single concept was represented by the words in a given list, and any one of the three words could be used to make the decision for all three words: If a subject knew that one instance was in List 2, for example, the other two instances would "follow along." I doubt if this happened; the major unit of memory for list identification was the concept name, not the instances. This is to say that had only a single instance of each concept been given the results would not have changed. Nor would the results have changed had the eight concept names been given on the test.

It remains possible, however, that the test given for the mixed lists could have placed these subjects at a disadvantage relative to those given the unmixed lists. Suppose that, on the test, the subject was given eight groups of three words each, each group representing words from one of the lists. The subject is told that the three words in each group were in fact in the same list. In this case, if one of the words was known to have been in a particular list, the other two would "follow along." In retrospect, I rather believe that this procedure would have been more appropriate as far as making the tests equivalent for the mixed and unmixed lists. But if the reasoning is correct, such a test could only reduce the difference between the two types of lists, thereby reducing the magnitude of the effect of semantic context on temporal coding. Also, it should be remembered that the two types of lists represented two extreme conditions. Undoubtedly, as a subject went about the learning of the mixed lists, concept names were implicitly elicited. These names would be quite useless for temporal coding and may have prevented the development of interrelationships within a list, which would occur had all eight lists been made up of unrelated words.

Correlational evidence. In Experiment 13, we found at best only weak evidence that the ability to learn the tasks was related to the establishment of valid temporal codes. In general, the same conclusion was reached for the present experiment. For the unmixed-list conditions, the correlations between number of words correctly recalled and the number of list identification errors were −.09, .18, and .15, none of which is statistically different from zero. For the mixed-list conditions, the values were −.37, −.36, and −.34. The consistency argues for a reliable relationship. It may be remembered that such a relationship was not found for the free-recall lists in Experiment 13.

Summary

The external-context tasks had no influence on temporal coding. I would repeat that there is no apparent reason why these external contexts should have influenced the temporal coding of the word lists. Even if subjects said to themselves, "Oh, that word is from the list that came right after that mirror-tracing task," they in addition would need to know where mirror tracing came in the series of eight tasks, if the word was to be correctly identified with its list.

I have argued that the true magnitude of the influence of semantic context on temporal coding is difficult to determine from the present data. It does seem reasonable to conclude that an effect was present, largely limited to the first two and last two lists.

EXPERIMENT 15

The purpose of Experiment 15 was to study the influence of semantic context on within-list temporal coding. The subject was presented lists of 25 words for a single study trial. Immediately after the presentation of a list, pairs of words were shown the subjects, and they were requested to choose the most recently presented word in each pair. Of the test pairs, only one was critical in evaluating the influence of semantic context. The logic of the experiment will be described with reference to these critical pairs.

The two target words in the test pairs were always neutral with respect to the context manipulation. These two words always occupied positions 7 and 18 in the 25-word lists. Context was introduced by placing four words from the same concept or category around a target word, with two preceding the target word and two following it. For example, the order would be *coats, socks, oxygen, pants, shoes* where *oxygen* was one of the two target words. It may be assumed that the concept name (in this case, clothing) would be implicitly elicited several times and, therefore, would be more readily remembered than would the target word. The neutral target word may become associated with the concept name. If it does, there are two potential sources of positioning information: information associated with the target word as such and information associated with the concept name. Thus, merely on a probability basis, position information may be better than if the context words were not present. Furthermore, if both target words were surrounded by distinctively different contexts, the position information for both of the words should be enhanced.

If conceptual context can facilitate acquisition of position information for a neutral word, then it should be possible to produce interference with this information. If both target words were surrounded by instances of the same concept, any positive effect of the context would be neutralized, and position information would have to be based on information accruing to the target words per se.

The above analysis determined the four basic conditions of the experiment:

Condition 0: No context around either target word
Condition 1: Context around one of the target words
Condition 2D: Different context around each target word
Condition 2S: Same context for both target words

The four conditions were represented by four independent groups of 20 subjects each. For each condition, the subjects were given 10 successive lists. The first list given the subjects in the four conditions illustrates the differences in list structure for the four conditions. These lists are shown in Table 6. It should be noted that the two target words (*book* and *river*) are the same for the four lists. In Condition 0, no conceptual context is presented for either target word. For Condition 1, four context words (kind of cloth) are positioned by the first target word, but there is no context for the second target word. For Condition 2D, both target words are set in conceptual contexts but the two contexts are different (kinds of cloth and birds). Finally, it can be seen that, for Condition 2S, four instances from the same category surround each target word.

Method

List construction. Eight words from each of 20 different categories were selected from the Battig-Montague (1969) norms. In most cases, these were the eight most frequently given responses to the category name. The words from these 20 categories were used to

TABLE 6

Illustration of the Lists Used in the Four Conditions of Experiment 15

Condition 0	Condition 1	Condition 2D	Condition 2S
1. engine	engine	engine	engine
2. oyster	oyster	oyster	oyster
3. forehead	forehead	forehead	forehead
4. recital	recital	recital	recital
5. butter	*satin*	*satin*	*satin*
6. lawn	*linen*	*linen*	*linen*
7. (book)	(book)	(book)	(book)
8. pledge	*silk*	*silk*	*silk*
9. telescope	*rayon*	*rayon*	*rayon*
10. ghost	ghost	ghost	ghost
11. monarch	monarch	monarch	monarch
12. algebra	algebra	algebra	algebra
13. disaster	disaster	disaster	disaster
14. meadow	meadow	meadow	meadow
15. worm	worm	worm	worm
16. party	party	*bluebird*	*cotton*
17. caravan	caravan	*hawk*	*nylon*
18. (river)	(river)	(river)	(river)
19. flag	flag	*sparrow*	*wool*
20. daylight	daylight	*eagle*	*dacron*
21. quart	quart	quart	quart
22. devil	devil	devil	devil
23. goblet	goblet	goblet	goblet
24. charter	charter	charter	charter
25. pressure	pressure	pressure	pressure

Note: Critical test words are in parentheses; context words are in italics.

implement the context manipulation. A further 20 category names were chosen from the norms; from each set of responses, a single high-frequency word was chosen. These 20 words were used as the 20 critical target words.

The lists for Condition 0 were constructed first. As a first step, the 20 critical target words were assigned randomly to a list and to one of the two positions (7 or 18) within the lists. From a variety of sources, 230 other words were brought together and were assigned randomly to the 230 positions remaining in the 10 lists. These 230 words had varying frequencies and were of several form classes. A word was not used in the pool if it fit into one of the 40 categories used to obtain the target words and context words.

The lists for Condition 1 were constructed next. From the sets of eight instances for each of 20 concepts, 10 were chosen randomly, and then four words from each set were chosen randomly. For the lists for Condition 1, the four words from a concept replaced the four neutral words for Condition 0 around one of the target words. Thus, as may be seen in Table 6, the four kinds of cloth were inserted in positions 5, 6, 8, and 9. On five of the 10 lists for Condition 1, the context words were used around the second target word, appearing in positions 16, 17, 19, and 20. Across the 10 lists for Condition 1, the context surrounded the target word in position 7 or position 18 as follows: 7, 18, 18, 7, 18, 7, 7, 18, 7, 18.

In constructing the context for the lists of Condition 1, 10 of the concepts were used. In making up the lists for Condition 2D, four instances from each of the remaining 10 concepts were used to provide the context for the 10 target words not given context in the lists of Condition 1. Finally, for Condition 2S, four additional instances of the 10 concepts used for the context for the lists of Condition 1 were placed around the target words not given context in Condition 1.

Study and test procedures.   All subjects were given a practice list before the 10 experimental lists. The subjects were fully instructed about all aspects of the procedure. They were asked to repeat the "gist" of the instructions to the experimenter to be sure there was no misunderstanding as to what was meant by the most recently presented word in a pair. The instructions did not include any information about the presence of conceptually related words in the lists.

The lists were presented for the single study trial at a 2-second rate. Immediately after the last word in the list was shown, the experimenter handed the test sheet for that list to the subject. This sheet contained five pairs of words, and the subject was required to circle the most recently presented word in each pair. The order of the five pairs on the test sheet was random, as were the left-right positions of the most recent word in the pair. As soon as the subject completed the unpaced test for a list, the next list was presented, and the steps were repeated for the series of lists.

One pair on each test sheet was, of course, the critical test pair. However, the other test pairs were not without interest for understanding temporal coding, and their characteristics will now be described.

1. Long lag. These pairs included one word from near the beginning of the list and one from near the end of the list. These long-lag pairs were separated by 19, 20, 21, or 22 other words. These words were identical for all conditions. The pair tested from the first lists (Table 6) consisted of *oyster* and *devil*, the lag being 19.

2. Short lag. The lag for these pairs was 0, 1, or 2 other words, and these test pairs were identical for all four types of lists. The two words were always taken from near the middle of the list, for example, *algebra* and *monarch* from the first lists.

3. Within. Within refers to recency tests for two words from the same concept. The lag was three, and always involved words from positions 5 and 9 or positions 16 and 20, with five from each across the ten lists. Of course, for Condition 0, these tests could not involve two words from the same concept, but the test for words in corresponding positions for Condition 0 served as control tests for the influence of concept identity on recency judgments. For the lists in Table 6, the test pair for Condition 0 was *telescope* and *butter*, and, for all other lists, the pair was *rayon* and *satin*.

4. Between. Between refers to recency tests for two words having a lag of 10 and both falling within the positions occupied by the context words. The test words came from either positions 6 and 17 or positions 8 and 19, each set being used for five lists. Again, the tests may be illustrated from the lists given in Table 6: Condition 0, *caravan* and *lawn*; Condition 1, *caravan* and *linen*; Condition 2D, *hawk* and *linen*; Condition 2S, *nylon* and *linen*. These tests allow comparisons of recency judgments for two words with a lag of 10, when both test words are from the same concept or are from different concepts. Judgments of the neutral words with a lag of 10 from Condition 0 provide a control baseline.

Results

The mean numbers of correct recency judgments for all item types under each condition are shown in Table 7. Because each mean is based on 10 tests, the values may be changed to percents by moving the decimal points one place to the right.

The results for the critical test pairs are given in the first row. Although the mean for the control (Condition 0) is lower than the other three means, statistically, the differences among the four means were not reliable, $F(3, 76) = 1.30$, $p > .05$. Even the largest difference (Condition 0 versus Condition 2D) was not reliable statistically ($t = 1.82$). Thus, although the judgments were correct about 75% of the time, the semantic context had no influence on the recency judgments for the pairs of neutral target words.

Table 7 shows that judgments for long-lag target pairs were far more accurate than for short-lag pairs, the latter being only slightly better than chance. The short-lag pairs provided further information of interest to which I will return at a later point.

An examination of the results for the within- and between-item types shows that they are a little complex, and it will be well to look at the statistics of the matter initially. When the four within means were tested, the differences just met the .05 level of significance,

TABLE 7

Mean Correct Recency Judgments for Conditions and Item Types
(Experiment 15)

Item types		Conditions			
	0	1	2D	2S	Mean
Critical	6.80	7.65	7.80	7.25	7.38
Short lag	5.75	5.30	5.60	5.50	5.54
Long lag	8.50	8.33	8.75	8.80	8.60
Within	6.25	7.60	7.60	7.15	7.15
Between	7.00	7.50	8.70	7.70	7.73
Mean:	6.86	7.28	7.69	7.28	

$F(3, 76) = 2.80$. The difference among the four means for the between type of tests was also reliable ($F = 3.32$). However, when both types of items were included in an analysis, the interaction between item types and conditions was far from significant ($F = 1.33$), although both main effects were reliable.

There are two facts from the above tests that are judged to be of systematic importance. First, in the within tests, performance was enhanced when a recency judgment was requested for two test words from the same concept cluster (Condition 0 versus the other three conditions). I believe this finding can be best understood in terms of serial learning. It is highly probable that a subject rehearsed the cluster of four related words in serial order, and the first word was usually known to have been the first word in the cluster. Given this knowledge, the fact that performance under Conditions 1, 2S, and 2D was superior to the performance under Condition 0 would be anticipated.

The second fact concerns the between type of test items. Performance under Condition 2D was far better than performance under Condition 0 ($t = 3.09$). This must mean that the two concept clusters, occurring in different sections of the list, facilitated the temporal coding of the instances of the concepts. That is, semantic context aided temporal coding for the words making up the context. The fact that interference was not observed in the between judgments for Condition 2S is taken to mean that the two clusters made up of instances of the same concept must have had ordering labels associated, such as first and second occurrence of instances of the same concept.

Changes in performance across the 10 lists were examined in detail. The only consistent finding that emerged involved the short-lag tests, where performance on the first five lists was at a chance level (50.8%) but increased to 60.0% on the last five lists. The short-lag tests included five tests of zero lag and five tests of pairs having lags of 1 or 2. The change in performance between the first five lists and the second five lists was examined separately for the zero lags and for the lags of 1 and 2 combined. The former increased from 45.6% to 62.5%, the latter from 54.2% to 56.3%. Overall, the performance was essentially equivalent for lags of zero and for lags of

1 and 2. This finding again suggests that serial learning may provide valid information for recency judgments. Whether the increase in performance over lists for pairs with lag zero was due to an intentional strategy of serial learning is not known.

Summary

The within-list manipulation of semantic context produced no effect on the temporal coding of the neutral target words. This was true in spite of the fact that there was evidence that the concept clusters aided the temporal coding of the instances of the concepts within the clusters. The logic of the experiment leads to the conclusion that the neutral target words embedded within the concept clusters did not become associated with the concept name. If such associations were established, the subjects did not use this information in making temporal judgments for the neutral target words.

EXPERIMENT 16

The final experiment to be reported had two purposes. In Chapter 2, it was pointed out that no studies on within-list temporal coding of verbal events have been done in which the number of different events falling between two targets was the independent variable. Of course, the usual lag manipulation represents a variation in the number of different events, but such manipulations are confounded with the true time between the targets. The first purpose of Experiment 16 was to keep the time between T1 and T2 constant while varying the number of different verbal events which occurred between them. Basically, this is a manipulation of event frequency to see if recency and lag judgments are influenced thereby.

One of the classical findings of research on the judgments of the duration of short temporal intervals is that an interval filled with an activity is judged to be shorter than an equivalent unfilled interval. Loosely speaking, filling an interval with many occurrences of the same event would correspond to an unfilled interval, and filling an interval with many different events, even of the same class, could be considered a filled interval. Whether the analogy is appropriate is clearly debateable. In any event, in the present experiment the number of different words falling between T1 and T2 within a list was the independent variable, there being three levels. Using the word *repetition* to indicate multiple occurrences of any frequency, we may speak of the density of repetition as the independent variable, and, in the present experiment, the three density levels will be called low, medium, and high. Following the presentation of the list for study, the subjects made recency judgments for T1 and T2, followed by a lag judgment. The empirical question is whether these measures of temporal coding will change systematically as a function of the density of repetition of the words falling between T1 and T2.

The second purpose of this experiment was to study the interrelationships among performances on three different memory tests taken after the study of a list. The memory tests, in addition to the temporal tests, included recall tests and frequency-judging tests. I have elsewhere discussed the potential value of tests of individual differences in theory formulation (Underwood, 1975). In the initial stages of our studies on temporal coding, we attempted to implement this approach. Two experiments were done on what we have called the integration of discrete units in recognition memory, when the units were presented at different points in time. For example, the two words *toothbrush* and *heartache* were presented at different positions in a long list. On the test, the subjects decided whether or not the word *toothache* had been presented in the study list. It had not been presented, of course, but could be derived from the elements (*tooth* and *ache*) of words actually presented. It seemed reasonable to presume that the likelihood of a subject accepting the derived word (a false alarm) would be related to the separation (lag) of the two inducing words in the study list. If this were so, we reasoned that subjects with good temporal coding would produce fewer false alarms than would subjects with poor temporal coding. The test of temporal coding that we constructed at that time was reported in this book as Experiment 2 (Chapter 1). As was noted, we were unable to demonstrate reliability in our measures; hence, we were unable to proceed with the plan. As it turned out, the lag in the recognition studies was not a relevant variable anyhow, and so the entire approach was completely aborted. The recognition data are presented elsewhere (Underwood, Kapelak, & Malmi, 1976).

In Experiments 13 and 14, learning measures were at best only marginally related to between-list temporal coding. In the present study, we are asking about the relationship for within-list measures, with the recency judgments used as the index of temporal coding. If, as we were beginning to suspect, recency judgments were based on some form of associative learning, a relationship between recall and recency judgments should emerge. If the density variable was found to influence the recency judgments, the magnitude of the effect among subjects may be related to the accuracy with which individuals perceive frequency differences.

Method

The task given the subjects may now be described. They were presented a list of 18 word triads (e.g., *ought-climb-funny*) for a single study trial at the relatively slow rate of six seconds per triad. Two of the 18 triads constituted the critical ones (T1 and T2) for determining the effect of density of repetition on recency and lag judgments. These two target triads always had a lag of seven; they were separated by seven other triads. The density of repetition varied among the words used to construct these seven intervening triads, the number of different words being 19, 14, and 9 for low, medium, and high density of repetition, respectively. The fully instructed subjects were given 10 experimental lists. After each list they: (1) made recency and lag judgments on two sets of two triads each (the critical target triads and two others having varying lags); (2) made frequency judgments for three single words, with true frequencies being 0, 1, 2, 3, and 4 when tests across all lists were considered; and (3) tried to complete a triad by recalling the missing word when two of the words were used as cues for recall.

List construction. The manipulation of density of repetition between T1 and T2 produced a difficult decision because of a potential confounding. Consider the difference between high density and low density of repetition among the 21 spaces in the seven triads falling between T1 and T2. If density is varied only among these triads and held constant among all others, then, of necessity, the total number of different words in the lists would vary. A proper solution would require (at the minimum) an orthogonal manipulation of the density of repetition among the seven critical triads between T1 and T2 and the density of repetition among the triads outside the seven critical ones. Because I did not choose to undertake an experiment of this magnitude without having some feel for the effects of the independent variable, I decided to live a little dangerously. The number of different words in all lists was kept constant for all conditions. With the condition of high density between T1 and T2 (List H), therefore, the density of repetition among the other triads was low. When the density of repetition between T1 and T2 was low (List L), the density of repetition among the other triads was high. It was hoped that the results for the condition with medium density of repetition (List M) between T1 and T2 would be of such nature as to help decide the source of the density producing differences (if such differences did indeed occur). In List M, the density of repetition was the same thoughout all sections of the list.

The practice list and each of the 10 experimental lists contained 18 triads (54 spaces) made up of 40 different words. A total of 446 five-letter words was selected. Of these, 421 were all of the A and AA words listed in Thorndike and Lorge (1944), except for contractions. This list was prepared by my colleague, Carl P. Duncan, to whom I am grateful for its use. The remaining 21 words had frequencies of 40–49 per million. Of the 446 words, 440 were required to construct the 11 lists. The remaining six words were used as new words on the frequency-judging tests for six of the lists. All assignments of words to function, list, and position in triads were done randomly. The only restriction was that a word could not occur more than once within a triad. Repetitions, therefore, always occurred among triads.

Within each list, there were at least eight unique triads, in that each word in them occurred only once in the list. Two of these eight unique triads occupied positions 1 and 18 (primacy and recency), and two were used as T1 and T2. These four unique triads had identical functions across all three types of lists (L, M, H). The positions of the four remaining unique triads differed for the three types of lists, as will be described shortly. The unique triads, including primacy and recency triads, were used in recall tests and recency-judgment tests.

It will be helpful to examine the lists. The first experimental lists of the three types are shown in Table 8. The construction of List L will be described first. The eight unique triads were first placed into position; these included the primacy and recency triads, T1 and T2, and four others falling in the seven positions between T1 and T2. Then, a single word (*about* in Table 8) was positioned three times in the remaining nine vacant spaces of the 21 falling between T1 and T2. The remaining six vacancies were filled by six different words. Thus, between T1 and T2, 19 different words occurred, of which 18 appeared once and one appeared three times. It was an intuitive belief that, for List L, the seven triads between T1 and T2 should not have zero repetition; thus, one word occurred three times. As a final step, the remaining nine words (of the 40 required for the list) were used to fill the 21 spaces in the seven triads occupying positions 2, 3, 14, 15, 16, and 17. In doing this, two words were used four times each, two words three times each, two words twice each, and three words once each. This provides a high density of repetition among the triads, which occurred before and after T1 and T2.

List H was constructed by simply moving the triads of List L. The triads in positions 5 through 11 were moved to positions 2, 3, 13, 14, 15, 16, and 17, and those occupying the latter positions in List L were moved to the positions between T1 and T2. List H, therefore, has a high density of repetition between T1 and T2, with a low density among the triads occurring before and after T1 and T2.

A slightly different method was used in the construction of List M. The primacy, recency, T1 and T2 triads were exactly the same as for the other two lists. The other four unique triads were positioned so that one occurred in the positions before T1, one in the positions after T2, and two within the seven positions between T1 and T2. This left 10 triads (30 spaces) to be inserted in the list, with five of the triads being between T1 and T2, and five before T1 and after T2. The 16 remaining words were used to fill these spaces, with two

TABLE 8
The First Experimental List for Each of the Three Conditions of
Experiment 16

List L	List M	List H
1. ought—climb—funny	ought—climb—funny	ought—climb—funny
2. match—table—fresh	shore—match—fresh	earth—sharp—about
3. fresh—shore—match	flock—scene—event	about—flock—event
4. *thick—check—small*	*thick—check—small*	*thick—check—small*
5. earth—sharp—about	treat—flock—watch	match—table—fresh
6. about—flock—event	awake—chose—grief	fresh—shore—match
7. throw—clear—treat	humor—event—treat	awake—early—grief
8. plain—cause—about	flock—aside—throw	match—shore—fresh
9. enter—scene—watch	table—early—steel	match—shore—grief
10. humor—aside—sugar	plain—sugar—clear	awake—chose—steel
11. never—bless—tooth	event—throw—enter	shore—awake—chose
12. *carry—round—empty*	*carry—round—empty*	*carry—round—empty*
13. awake—early—grief	cause—never—plain	throw—clear—treat
14. match—shore—fresh	event—clear—enter	plain—cause—about
15. match—shore—grief	about—earth—sharp	enter—scene—watch
16. awake—chose—steel	bless—flock—cause	humor—aside—sugar
17. shore—awake—chose	throw—tooth—clear	never—bless—tooth
18. under—field—linen	under—field—linen	under—field—linen

Note: The critical target items, T1 and T2, are in italics.

words occurring four times each, two words three times each, four words twice each, and eight words once each. The result was that the density of repetition was constant throughout the list as a whole, with the average number of words (across lists) used in the triads between T1 and T2 being 14. Thus, Lists L, M, and H had 19, 14, and 9 different words, respectively, falling between T1 and T2.

For the lists in Table 8, T1 and T2 occupy positions 4 and 12. To avoid the remote possibility that the subjects might learn to expect a recency test for the two triads in these positions, positions 5 and 13 and positions 6 and 14 were used for T1 and T2 in other lists. This was randomly determined. Positions 4 and 12 and positions 6 and 14 were each used in three lists for T1 and T2, and positions 5 and 13 identified T1 and T2 in four lists.

Tests.   Recency tests (and the corresponding lag judgments) and recall tests were always conducted using the unique triads. For the recency tests, T1 and T2 were always tested, of course. In addition, two other triads were used to form a second recency test for each list. The lag for these varied from list to list across the 10 lists and also differed for Lists L, M, and H. Three triads were used in the recall tests for each list; hence, a total of 30 correct responses was possible. Frequency judgments were made for three words in each list (in six lists, the third word was a new word). Across the 10 lists, the 30 judgments were made for six words at each of the five frequencies (0, 1, 2, 3, 4).

A test sheet was given the subject immediately after the last triad was shown on the study trial. The tests on the sheets were always in the order of recall, recency and lag, and frequency. However, the subject could make the decisions in any order he chose. For the recall tests, two words were given, with a blank identifying the missing word: noise-   -stood. For the three triads tested after each list, the missing word occurred once in each position. For the recency tests, the subjects were asked to circle the most recently occurring triad, and then to circle a number from 0 through 18, to indicate the lag. The order of the two triads on the tests varied randomly. Three words were given for the frequency judgments, with the subject required to circle a number (0, 1, 2, 3, 4) to indicate the number of times each had occurred.

The tests were unpaced, but a maximum of 2 minutes was imposed to prevent the subjects from spending an inordinate amount of time trying to recall the missing words. It should be noted that the tests for a list never involved the same words or the same triads; that is, the words in a triad given for a recency judgment never occurred in either the recall or frequency tests. For some of the recall tests and for some of the noncritical recency tests, the primacy and recency triads were used. In effect, then, the subject could expect to be tested in some manner for words from every triad in the list.

Procedure and subjects.   Complete instructions concerning the nature of study lists and the nature of the tests were given before the practice list. The subject then repeated the gist of the instructions to the experimenter. After the tests on the practice list, any further questions were answered and the study trial for the first experimental list followed. The entire procedure required about 50 minutes.

Three groups of 36 subjects each were assigned to the three lists by a block randomized schedule.

Results

Critical target words.   Each subject made 10 recency judgments for T1 and T2, these target triads being identical for the three list types. The mean numbers of correct judgments were 7.25, 7.75, and 8.05 for Lists L, M, and H, respectively. These values suggest that correct responding increased as the density of repetition between T1 and T2 increased, but the effect lacked statistical reliability, $F(2, 105) = 2.36$, $p > .05$. Although it is remotely possible that contrary effects could have been produced by the reciprocal density (as discussed earlier), the most reasonable conclusion seems to be that the repetition variable was of little consequence for the recency judgments.

The true lag for the critical target words was seven. The mean lag judgments were 5.73, 5.54, and 5.52 for Lists L, M, and H, respectively ($F < 1$). The lag judgments were obviously not influenced by the repetition variable. An examination was made of the recency judgments and of the lag judgments from list to list. The recency judgments did not change in any systematic way across the 10 lists. The lag judgments increased a small amount, the increase being largely confined to the first three lists.

The lag judgments and recency judgments for the critical items have been examined in several ways, and all point toward two conclusions: The subjects had only a vague notion of the true lag, and lag judgments were unrelated to recency judgments. The following facts have led to these conclusions:

1. The standard deviations for the 10 lag judgments were calculated for each subject. To illustrate the outcome, it was found that for List M these standard deviations varied between .98 and 4.03. Individual lag judgments varied between zero and 18, the two extremes allowed the subjects.

2. Lag judgments were essentially equivalent for correct and incorrect recency decisions.

3. On the sixth list, T2 (occurring as the thirteenth triad) consisted of *upper-birth-lover*. For whatever reason, salacious or otherwise, 106 of the 108 subjects gave a correct recency judgment for the pair of triads. For the fifth list, only 76 of the 108 subjects made a correct recency decision for the critical targets. Yet, the mean lag judgments were almost identical for the two cases: 5.95 and 5.96.

4. The mean deviation of the lag judgments from the true lag for each subject was correlated with the number of correct recency judgments. For the three lists the correlations were .03, .17, and −.23.

Other recency and lag judgments.   The subjects also made recency and lag judgments for 10 other pairs of target triads. Some of these triads had occupied the first or last position in the list, and the lags varied from 1 through 14. For all of the lists combined, the mean number of correct recency judgments was 8.09. For each subject a rank-order correlation was calculated between true lag and estimated lag for the 10 tests. Of the 108 correlations, 81 were positive and 27 were negative. The overall mean correlation was .26, which, while reliably different from zero, does not indicate a very substantial relationship between true lag and the lag estimates.

Recall.   Each subject had the opportunity to recall 30 words. The number recalled varied between 0 and 28, with a mean of 10.16 (33.9%). The three groups did not differ reliably. The locus of the missing word (first, second, or third position in the triad) did not influence recall, the values being 33.5, 32.8, and 33.6%, respectively, for the three positions. An analysis of recall as a function of the position of the triad in the series of 18 showed there to be no primacy effect. The recency effect was limited to the last triad.

Frequency judgments.   The subjects estimated the frequency of 30 different words, six at each of the five frequency levels (0, 1, 2, 3, 4). They were required to restrict their estimates to the values 0 through 4. Overall, the judgments showed the usual overestimation for low frequencies and underestimation for high frequencies. The product—moment correlation between true and estimated frequency for the 30 words was used to reflect each individual's sensitivity to frequency differences. The mean correlations were .69, .69, and .66 for Lists L, M, and H, respectively. Only one of the 108 subjects had a negative correlation.

Correlations among tasks.   It will be remembered that each subject made 20 recency judgments, 10 on the critical targets and 10 on targets having varying lags. We had hoped that reliability of the recency judgments could be demonstrated by correlating the number of correct responses on each set of 10 judgments, although we realized that chance factors in the two-choice decisions could make this troublesome. The correlations were positive, but low (.28, .34, .07, for L, M, and H). Nevertheless, believing that summing the number correct for both sets would reduce the role of chance factors in the individual scores, we proceeded to determine the correlations across tasks. As indicated, the total correct for the recency judgments was used as one measure. The other two measures were total recall, and the product—moment correlations calculated from the frequency judgments. Each of the individual correlations was transformed to a z' value before calculating the correlations for the frequency judgments across tasks.

Initially, the correlations among the scores on the three tasks were determined for each list. These correlations were then transformed to the z' measure, averaged for the three lists, and then retransformed to r. The correlations will be given for each list in the order of L, M, and H, with the average correlation in parenthesis: recency x recall, .70, .56, .34 (.55); recency x frequency, .37, .60, .27 (.42); recall x frequency, .58, .73, .23 (.55). These data support the conclusion that within-list recency judgments are mediated by attributes that are related to those involved in recall and in frequency discrimination, particularly the former. It seems fairly certain that given more stability in the recency scores for individuals than was true in the present data, the relationship between recency scores and recall scores would be high.

Discussion

The independent variable, repetition density, had no clear effect on recency judgments. If, as the cumulative evidence is beginning to suggest, recency judgments are based on associative learning, then perhaps the repetition density would not be expected to be of importance. I will leave to the next chapter some speculations as to how associative learning may mediate recency judgments. It was probably more reasonable to believe that repetition density would influence lag judgments more than it would influence recency judgments. But, again, the cumulative evidence is pointing to the fact that lag judgments are largely guesses; lag judgments cannot be handled with any degree of precision by the memory attributes available to the subjects.

SUMMARY

The description of the 16 experiments designed to study factors influencing temporal coding is complete. It seems that a ghastly habit afflicts most experimental psychologists as they prepare their manuscripts. These manuscripts are usually sprinkled liberally (to use a cliche) with the most deadening batch of cliches ever used in communications among reasonably intelligent people. Some examples: (1) "More research is needed"; (2) "The results are more complex than anticipated"; (3) "This is a progress report"; (4) "The exploratory nature of the experiment is obvious"; (5) "Future experiments should clarify the matter." I herewith declare all of these to be appropriate for the experiments reported here.

6
Interim

In theory, it would seem, all research has a natural or logical ending, namely, that point at which the understanding of a phenomenon is complete. In practice, there is no end to research; there are only pauses. Solutions for nature's puzzles occur at a given level of analysis, and, after a pause, the work moves in new directions or to different levels of analysis. I rather doubt that any scientist ever became unemployed because his understanding of a phenomenon was complete or total.

A pause in the research represents the natural point for the final stage of any major research effort, that of making the findings public through the written report. Yet, for many reasons (not all of which are easily defended), research is frequently published even if it has not reached a logical point of pause. Sometimes we even commit ourselves to a report before we know fully about the characteristics of the data upon which the report is to be based. I mention these matters to reveal my awareness of the fact that a pause, rather than occurring as a natural or logical ending to a series of studies, is sometimes reluctantly declared.

This final chapter will be concerned first with a summary of the basic findings in the three areas of temporal coding that have been identified: within-list, between-list short term, and between-list in the long-term studies using the proactive inhibition paradigm. These summaries will be interwoven with: (1) a discussion of problems and issues that seem to be associated with differences in methods of studying temporal coding; and (2) some explanatory notions.

WITHIN-LIST TEMPORAL CODING

Methods and Findings

Three sets of operations have been used to measure within-list temporal coding. First, a list of words is presented for a study trial after which the subjects are asked to identify the position held by each item on the study trial. Experiments 4 and 5 used this method. Second, after a list is presented for study, the subjects are given pairs of words from the list and are asked to choose the most recently occurring word in each pair. In the present series, Experiments 2, 11, 15, and 16 used this method, which I have called the discrete-list method. In the third procedure, the continuous-list procedure, the subjects are shown a long series of words and, periodically during the showing, are asked for recency judgments on pairs of words. This technique was not used in experiments reported here. In the second and third methods, lag judgments may be requested in addition to, or in lieu of, recency judgments.

One might think, as I did originally, that these methods must be at least roughly equivalent for the purpose of measuring temporal coding. Having completed the studies and having examined the results they produced in conjunction with the results of other investigators, I am forced to conclude that I was somewhat naive about the matter. I should have known better: Having been trained in a functionalist atmosphere, I had no reason to forget the oft-repeated dictum, "The influence of an independent variable may vary as a function of the methods used to investigate it." It now appears to me that one of the central problems that emerges is that these methods do not always yield equivalent estimates of the effects of some independent variables. I will review some of the evidence leading to this conclusion.

I have earlier described the first problem. When subjects are asked to make position judgments of individual words after a long list is given for study, their decisions show a clear relationship with true position. However, when pairs of words are taken from the list and lag judgments requested, no relationship is evident between the judgments and true lag (Hintzman, Summers & Block, 1975). If subjects had knowledge that allowed them to make reliable position judgments, why cannot they make reliable lag judgments? More concretely, if they could with some accuracy identify the position of T1 and T2, why cannot a difference score be derived to make the lag judgment?

Obviously, subjects do not seem to be able to translate position information for two items into lag information; to be asked about the number of other words which fell between T1 and T2 must mean something quite different from being asked about the position each held in the list. In conjunction with this problem, it should also be remembered that subjects do not operate logically with regard to lag judgments. Logically, if a subject doesn't know whether T1 or T2 was most recent, it would be proper to assign a short lag. That is, it would be logical if the subjects "believe" that lack of valid information for making a lag judgment is because T1 and T2 occurred close together. Either they have not internalized the presumed positive correlation between apparent recency and lag or, if they have, realize it is fallible.

A second problem arises because of the lack of relationship between lag and lag judgments in our studies. It is true that our experiments usually showed a slight and statistically significant lag effect (Experiments 2 and 11), but to find that the subjects could not improve lag judgments over trials makes it highly likely that the small lag effects are the result of correlated information. For example, in Experiment 16, there was a positive correlation between lag and lag judgments for noncritical items, but it seems possible that this was due to primacy and recency information for the list. Lag and lag judgments have been related in the continuous-list procedure when the judgments were made for repeated items (e.g., Lockhart, 1969). In Experiment 11, repeated words were used and a slight relationship was apparent, but again there was no increase in the relationship across the three trials. Small effects have also been found for repeated words in the discrete-list procedure when the lists were long, but no effects were found for unrelated words (Hintzman, Summers, & Block, 1975). I think it becomes clear why I now lean toward the position that, in the experimental situations with which we work, lag judgments are simply not appropriate for indexing temporal coding. I restrict this to the experimental situation because the evidence from Experiment 1 showed that, when lags are measured in months for naturalistic memories, lag and perceived separation are related.

The relationship between lag and recency judgments also seems to depend upon method; correct recency judgments in the discrete within-list method are not importantly determined by lag length.

Again, in Experiment 2, there was a slight effect of lag on recency judgments; in Experiment 11, this same slight relationship was found for some of the conditions. Several bits of evidence from the judgments on the critical items of Experiment 16 indicated that recency judgments and lag judgments were unrelated and that the latter judgments were largely guesswork. On the other hand, in the continuous-list procedure, correct recency decisions clearly have been shown to increase as lag increases. For example, Galbraith (1975a) found this to be true with subjects from the third grade, from the sixth grade, and from college, for both words and pictures.

Thus, it appears that there are several problems posed by factual disagreements, which apparently result from differences in the methods by which the facts were recorded. In order to see if some resolution of these problems can be realized, I will now turn to some theoretical notions that I have found to be of some use in thinking about temporal coding. The first theoretical idea is the recency principle.

The Recency Principle

I have pointed out in Chapter 2 that we are able to deal with verbal units being studied at the moment without serious problems produced by intrusion of other units of the same class, or intrusion of units recently acquired in the same situation. This has been said to be due to a selector mechanism. For the present, I will speak of this capacity to isolate the material of the moment to be the recency principle. As a first step in a more thorough explication of the principle, I want to look at it within the temporal coding context.

Suppose I present the subject a series of verbal units using the continuous-list procedure. Immediately after presenting T2, I show the subjects T1 and T2 and ask which was most recent. It seems beyond doubt that we would get 100% correct recency judgments, regardless of where T1 occurred in the list. Why would performance be so high? Some might suggest that it results from the fact that T2 was in short-term memory and T1 was not. However, I suspect that if the T1−T2 lag was one item, so that both T1 and T2 would be said to be in short-term memory by the usual convention, the recency judgments would still be 100% correct. The percentage will surely fall as the interval between T2 and the test increases. The recency principle is as just stated; immediately after the perception of an item, temporal information for that item relative to other items coming before it is perfect, but as time passes the information available becomes less and less reliable.

A recency principle, or some principle similar to it, seems to me to be an absolute necessity as a means of accounting for orderliness in behavior dependent upon the memory system. For example, I do not see how it is possible to generate spontaneously a series of sentences that are logically ordered as to meaning, unless we can distinguish between the last sentence produced and the other sentences produced prior to it. Indeed, I suspect we must distinguish between the last two or three sentences generated and those generated earlier, if the output is to be orderly. Consider some other situations. On aural free recall, we can be quite sure that, if a subject produces a word twice, there will be a number of other words separating the two occurrences. If we ask a subject to name as many different instances of a large category as rapidly as he can think of them, I would be confident that the probability of repetition would be related to the number of intervening items produced.

In spite of the fact that I believe a recency principle is a necessity, there are problems attending its use as an explanatory concept in the context of temporal coding in general. Some of these problems must be mentioned:

1. Although it is remotely possible that recency discrimination has a fixed rate of return to a baseline, it is more likely that the rate of loss of recency information is influenced by events that occur after the moment that recency is established at its maximum level. Ignorance concerning the time parameters may lead to an undisciplined use of recency as an explanatory concept.

2. I have no objections to the concept of strength when it is used to describe the relationship between number of repetitions of an item and the probability of recall or recognition. However, the recency principle is not a strength theory in that sense, although predictions from a strength theory and a recency principle may overlap.

3. The recency principle may be viewed entirely in the abstract. This is to say it may be postulated without identifying the particular content of the memory that is involved. This is out of step with the general orientation within which I have been working, the orientation involving attributes of memory that are identifiable by analytical experiments. The fact is I have not been able to remove the recency principle from its abstract position. If, then, I speak of the recency attribute, it will be recognized that I am merely using an alternative way of speaking about the abstract recency principle.

With the recency principle before us, I will now list the assumptions which will be used to see if some resolution of the problems mentioned earlier can be achieved, as well as to account for other basic facts that have evolved from the experiments on within-list encoding. As will be seen, except for the recency principle, the assumptions are really nothing but strong empirical generalizations.

Basic Assumptions

1. The recency principle identifies the only mechanism that provides direct age information about memories.
2. All other temporal codes are derived from associative learning.
3. Temporal codes can be established by associative processes only when a known ordering system is involved in the associative learning.
4. The lag between two memories as manipulated in the laboratory is irrelevant to temporal coding.

Associative Learning and Temporal Coding

It is not my intent to explain how associative learning occurs. Associative learning will be taken as a givens and the discussion will revolve around the particular paradigms of associative learning that seem to me to be involved in establishing temporal codes.

As was argued in Chapter 2, serial learning provides a basis for inferring order of events. This conclusion seems so self-evident that we did not seek analytical evidence on the matter. And, since serial learning is of small consequence for the explanatory problems faced in the present data, I will dispense with any further discussion of it.

A paradigm of associative learning that I believe to be of great importance in establishing temporal codes is what I will call two-category classification learning. Not much work has been done with this paradigm, but some of the evidence available is quite startling. I will illustrate this by reviewing a study performed by Ghatala, Levin, and Subkoviak (1975). Children from the fifth and sixth grades were shown 80 different words at a 4-second rate. Half of the words were underlined, and the underlining was a signal for the subject to pronounce that word. When the word was not under-lined, the subject remained silent. After a single study trial, the words were presented at a 3-second rate, and the subjects were asked to identify the words that they had pronounced on the study trial ("Yes") and those they had not pronounced ("No"). The subjects were able to respond correctly to.80% of the words. In view of the fact that some of the words might not even have been recognized on the test, the learning of the proper classification for each of the words must be considered to be quite high.

Now, we need to consider within-list experiments such as Experiments 15 and 16. In these experiments there were two critical targets, one in the early part of the list, one in the latter part. Let us assume that the subjects classified the items into two or three categories, such as "first part," "middle," and "last part." Recency judgments may then be mediated by this information on the test when T1 and T2 are shown and a recency judgment required. The critical target words occurred in the first and last parts, and, if such verbal labels (or similar ones) were associated with the target words, correct recency judgments should have resulted. Furthermore, the classification provides no information for a lag judgment or, at best, only a crude lag judgment. In Experiment 15, recency judgments were requested for short-lag pairs, which had occurred in the middle of the list; performance was only slightly above chance. Even a three-category form of learning would not mediate correct recency judgments for such tests, although, when the lag was zero, serial associations could produce correct responding.

When recency judgments are found to be correlated with lag, it is my belief that it results from a classification implying order for one or both of the target items. For example, in Experiment 16, there was some evidence that lag and recency judgments were correlated for the noncritical recency tests. The long lags inevitably involved a triad that was near the end of the list and a triad near the beginning of the list. Under these circumstances, a subject could reach a correct recency decision by having classified only one of the targets. Short lags, on the other hand, generally involved two triads that might normally be expected to be given the same classification.

The independence of lag and recency judgments was most apparent in Experiment 11. In the basic condition of this experiment, the subjects studied 24 sets of $A-B$, $A-D$ pairs, with the lag varying between the pairs having a common stimulus term. There were other conditions in this experiment, but I assume the same explanation will cover all of them. The results showed that the subjects had no gain in lag discrimination across three trials, and, although correct recency judgments increased across trials, lag did not influence these recency judgments. The quantitative aspects of the learning should be reviewed. On the first trial, the subjects were never correct more than 60% of the time under any condition, with chance being 50%. On the third trial, performance was never higher than 75%. Thus, in any absolute sense, performance was not high initially, and correct responding increased slowly.

Because the items of different lags were scattered throughout the list and there was no evidence that position in the list influenced correct responding, it is obvious that associative classification learning based on list position would not mediate correct responding. However, a two-category classification based on "first" and "second," corresponding to $A-B$ and $A-D$, could be learned and could be independent of the lag between two pairs. Furthermore, correct recency judgments could be made if the subject learned the appropriate classification for either of the two test members.

The assumption that associative classification learning is primarily responsible for recency judgments, hence for temporal coding, in the discrete within-list experiments is consistent with the finding that recall and recency judgments were positively correlated in Experiment 16. This is in contrast to the between-list studies of temporal coding where it appears that associative learning ability is at best only weakly associated with the temporal coding that occurs under incidental learning conditions.

As a final step, we need to return to the contradictions in fact that were listed earlier and seem to be associated with the method of studying within-list temporal coding. Do the assumptions made about the processes involved in temporal coding clarify the apparent contradictions? The answer seems to be that only a modest amount of clarification is added. One of the contradictions centered on the fact that, in the continuous-list procedure, lag is related to recency judgments, whereas it is not in the discrete-list technique. I see no reasonable way by which associative classification learning can be invoked to account for recency judgments in the continuous-list procedure. In most of the studies using this paradigm the T2—test interval is relatively short, for example, 3 to 5 items. I must assume that, within such short intervals, the recency attribute is involved. The longer the lag, the greater the difference in the recency attribute for the two test items. When the T2—test interval is long and lag and recency judgments are still shown to be related (e.g., Lockhart, 1969), the recency principle cannot reasonably be applied. In fact, I have no account for such results, other than to fall back on the weak idea that they may occur because the subject fails to recognize some of the T1 test items and that this failure is directly related both to the interval between T1 and T2 and the interval between T2 and the test. The T2 item gets chosen by default, so to speak.

A problem that I have been quite unable to solve has to do with the fact that position judgments for items in a long list are made with considerable accuracy, whereas recency judgments for pairs of items from the list reflect no evidence of temporal discrimination. Even if the position judgments are made on the basis of crude classification learning, pairs of items with long lags should be distinguishable on the basis of having been in different classes. Position judgments might be mediated by frequency information identified in terms of the number of items that had occurred prior to the occurrence of a particular item. But, again, it is difficult to see why such information cannot be translated into a recency judgment that would differ as a function of lag. It may be that the subject cannot transform information concerning position of individual items (however derived) into position differences. Clearly, as an experimenter, I could take position judgments from a long list and derive recency judgments that would be related to lag, but apparently the subject cannot do this when asked directly. I have to leave this issue in the unfinished-business category. This is another way of saying that the theory that has been sketched will not handle all of the available evidence.

BETWEEN-LIST TEMPORAL CODING: SHORT TERM

With Experiment 15, we were unable to demonstrate any effect of conceptual context on within-list temporal coding of neutral words. This was true in spite of the finding that temporal coding of the concept instances was facilitated. Experiments 13 and 14 asked about the role of context on temporal coding *between* lists of words. These results will be summarized. In Experiment 13, the context was identified with particular processes underlying learning of a given type of task. To provide a potential ordering system, the list numbers were given with high frequency to maximize the possibility of establishing associations among list numbers, words within the list, and process context. It was assumed that these associations would be less well established when the process context was the same across lists than when it was different. The data gave strong support to the notion, but an odd finding was that for only half the subjects was list identification performance aided by the different contexts. In Experiment 14, two types of context were manipulated: external context and conceptual context, the latter represented by having the conceptual context unique for each list or mixed across lists. External context had no influence on temporal coding; conceptual context did.

The learning underlying the temporal coding for Experiments 13 and 14 was not appreciably related to the subjects' abilities to learn the lists per se, nor was an item that was learned easily any more likely to be identified with the appropriate list than was one that was difficult to learn. The performance test for temporal coding was incidental, in that the subjects did not know that they would be tested for their knowledge of list membership of the items. Thus, the subject did not intentionally set about to devise a calendarlike system to serve as an ordering device for the lists, although previous work (Zimmerman & Underwood, 1968) indicates that the results would not have changed had the subjects been fully informed. Indeed, the results for Experiment 14 are very similar to the results obtained by Zimmerman and Underwood for both intentional and incidental conditions.

When list numbers are not provided in the learning context for several successive lists, crude classification learning will still occur. That is, a subject will implicitly provide labels that give order information for some of the lists, particularly the initial lists. The association between labels and the list items will be maximal when the items in a list can be characterized as a whole, (e.g., as animal names). If a subject does not know how many lists there are in the series, no label can be applied to the last list as it is being learned. Therefore, when temporal judgments for the items in the last list are better than for those in the preceding list, we must assume that the recency principle is responsible.

BETWEEN-LIST TEMPORAL CODING: LONG TERM

In the studies that were responsible for my interest in temporal coding in general, differences in proactive inhibition were used as the index of differences in temporal coding. Experimenter pain could have also been used as the index. I believe our studies have made it nearly certain that differences in word characteristics are critically involved in determining whether or not the temporal separation in the learning of two interfering lists will influence the order information for the two lists. Idle thoughts about this matter, however, have sometimes led to the frightening idea that some far more simple difference between the 1968 and 1971 Lists has been responsible and that my closeness to the experiments has blinded me to it. I would hope this is true and that someone with a different perspective will see it. I hope it is true because I believe that to take the gross differences between the two sets of lists as a point of departure for analytical research would be like clearing a forest with only a hatchet as a tool. In both situations, stamina is likely to be more useful than insight.

References

Abra, J. C. List differentiation and the point of interpolation in free-recall learning. *Journal of Verbal Learning and Verbal Behavior*, 1970, *9*, 665–671.

Abra, J. C. List differentiation and forgetting. In C. P. Duncan, L. Sechrest, & A. W. Melton (Eds.), *Human memory*. New York: Appleton-Century-Crofts, 1972.

Alin, L. H. Proactive inhibition as a function of the time interval between the learning of the two tasks and the number of prior lists. *Journal of Verbal Learning and Verbal Behavior*, 1968, *7*, 1024–1029.

Battig, W. F., & Montague, W. E. Category norms for verbal items in 56 categories: A replication and extension of the Connecticut norms. *Journal of Experimental Psychology Monograph*, 1969, *80* (3, Pt. 2).

Berlyne, D. E. Effects of spatial order and inter-item interval on recall of temporal order. *Psychonomic Science*, 1966, *6*, 375–376.

Brelsford, J., Jr., Freund, R., & Rundus, D. Recency judgments in a short-term memory task. *Psychonomic Science*, 1967, *8*, 247–248.

Carroll, J. B., & White, M. N. Age-of-acquisition norms for 220 picturable nouns. *Journal of Verbal Learning and Verbal Behavior*, 1973, *12*, 563–576.

Deese, J. Frequency of usage and number of words in free recall: the role of association. *Psychological Reports*, 1960, *7*, 337–344.

Ekstrand, B. R., Wallace, W. P., & Underwood, B. J. A frequency theory of verbal-discrimination learning. *Psychological Review*, 1966, *73*, 566–578.

Falkenberg, P. R. Recall improves in short-term memory the more recall context resembles learning context. *Journal of Experimental Psychology*, 1972, *95*, 39–47.

Flexser, A. J., & Bower, G. H. How frequency affects recency judgments: A model for recency discrimination. *Journal of Experimental Psychology*, 1974, *103*, 706–716.

Fozard, J. L. Apparent recency of unrelated pictures and nouns presented in the same sequence. *Journal of Experimental Psychology*, 1970, *86*, 137–143.

Galbraith, R. C. A developmental investigation of the independence of attributes of memory. Unpublished doctoral dissertation, Northwestern University, 1975. (a)

Galbraith, R. C. On the independence of attributes of memory. *Journal of Experimental Psychology: Human Learning and Memory*, 1975, *1*, 23–30. (b)

Galbraith, R. C. The effects of frequency and recency on judgments of frequency and recency. *American Journal of Psychology*, 1976, in press.

Ghatala, E. S., Levin, J. R., & Subkoviak, M. J. Rehearsal strategy effects in children's discrimination learning: Confronting the crucible. *Journal of Verbal Learning and Verbal Behavior*, 1975, *14*, 398–407.

Gibson, E. J., & Levin, H. *The psychology of reading*. Cambridge, Mass.: MIT Press, 1975.

Godden, D. R., & Baddeley, A. D. Context-dependent memory in two natural environments: On land and underwater. *British Journal of Psychology*, 1975, *66*, 325–331.

Goodwin, C. J., & Bruce, D. Temporal dating and single-trial free recall. *American Journal of Psychology*, 1972, *85*, 597–604.

Guenther, R. K., & Linton, M. Mechanisms of temporal coding. *Journal of Experimental Psychology: Human Learning and Memory*, 1975, *1*, 182–187.

Harcum, E. R. *Serial learning and para-learning*. New York: Wiley, 1975.

Hasher, L., & Johnson, M. K. Interpretive factors in forgetting. *Journal of Experimental Psychology: Human Learning and Memory*, 1975, *1*, 567–575.

Hicks, R. E., & Young, R. K. Part-whole transfer in free recall as a function of word class and imagery. *Journal of Experimental Psychology*, 1973, *101*, 100–104.

Hinrichs, J. ·V. A two-process memory-strength theory for judgments of recency. *Psychological Review*, 1970, *77*, 223–233.

Hinrichs, J. V., & Buschke, H. Running missing scan: Perception of oldest member in serial presentations. *Psychonomic Science*, 1970, *19*, 125–126.

Hintzman, D. L., & Block, R. A. Repetition and memory: Evidence for a multiple-trace hypothesis. *Journal of Experimental Psychology*, 1971, *88*, 297–306.

Hintzman, D. L., & Block, R. A. Memory for the spacing of repetitions. *Journal of Experimental Psychology*, 1973, *99*, 70–74.

Hintzman, D. L., Summers, J. J., & Block, R. A. Spacing judgments as an index of study-phase retrieval. *Journal of Experimental Psychology: Human Learning and Memory*, 1975, *1*, 31–40.

Hintzman, D. L., & Waters, R. M. Interlist and retention intervals in list discrimination. *Psychonomic Science*, 1969, *17*, 357–358.

Hintzman, D. L., & Waters, R. M. Recency and frequency as factors in list discrimination. *Journal of Verbal Learning and Verbal Behavior*, 1970, *9*, 218–221.

Ihalainen, V. J. The interference theory of forgetting. *Journal of Psychology*, 1968, *70*, 227–239.

Kappauf, W. E., & Payne, M. C. Performance-decrement at an observer-paced task. *American Journal of Psychology*, 1959, *72*, 443–446.

Keppel, G. Facilitation in short- and long-term retention of paired associates following distributed practice in learning. *Journal of Verbal Learning and Verbal Behavior*, 1964, *3*, 91–111.

Kincaid, J. P., & Wickens, D. D. Temporal gradient of release from proactive inhibition. *Journal of Experimental Psychology*, 1970, *86*, 313–316.

Kornblum, S. (Ed.) *Attention and performance IV*. New York: Academic Press, 1973.

Lassen, G. L., Daniel, T. C., & Bartlett, N. R. Judgments of recency for pictures and words. *Journal of Experimental Psychology*, 1974, *102*, 795–798.

Linton, M. Memory for real-world events. In D. A. Norman & D. E. Rumelhart (Eds.), *Explorations in cognition*. San Francisco: W. H. Freeman, 1975.

Lockhart, R. S. Recency discrimination predicted from absolute lag judgments. *Perception and Psychophysics*, 1969, *6*, 42–44.

Maslow, A. H. The effect of varying time intervals between acts of learning with a note on proactive inhibition. *Journal of Experimental Psychology*, 1934, *17*, 141–144.

McCrystal, T. J. List differentiation as a function of time and test order. *Journal of Experimental Psychology*, 1970, *83*, 220–223.

McGeoch, J. A. Forgetting and the law of disuse. *Psychological Review*, 1932, *39*, 352–370.

Melton, A. W. Implications of short-term memory for a general theory of memory. *Journal of Verbal Learning and Verbal Behavior*, 1963, *2*, 1–21.

Peterson, L. R. Search and judgment in memory. In B. Kleinmuntz (Ed.), *Concepts and the structure of memory*. New York: Wiley, 1967.

Peterson, L. R., & Gentile, A. Proactive interference as a function of time between tests. *Journal of Experimental Psychology*, 1965, *70*, 473–478.

Peterson, L. R., Johnson, S. T., & Coatney, R. The effect of repeated occurrences on judgments of recency. *Journal of Verbal Learning and Verbal Behavior*, 1969, *8*, 591–596.

Proctor, R. W., & Ambler, B. A. Effects of rehearsal strategy on memory for spacing and frequency. *Journal of Experimental Psychology: Human Learning and Memory*, 1975, *1*, 640–647.

Saufley, W. H., Jr. Memory for serial position. *Journal of Verbal Learning and Verbal Behavior,* 1975, *14*, 418–429.

Shuell, T. J., & Keppel, G. Retroactive inhibition as a function of learning method. *Journal of Experimental Psychology,* 1967, *75*, 457–463.

Squire, L. R., Chace, P. M., & Slater, P. C. Assessment of memory for remote events. *Psychological Reports,* 1975, *37*, 223–234.

Thorndike, E. L., & Lorge, I. *The teacher's wordbook of 30,000 words.* New York: Bureau of Publications, Teachers College, 1944.

Twedt, H. M., & Underwood, B. J. Mixed vs. unmixed lists in transfer studies. *Journal of Experimental Psychology,* 1959, *58*, 111–116.

Tzeng. O. J. L. The precedence effect in verbal information processing. *American Journal of Psychology,* 1976, in press.

Underwood, B. J. Attributes of memory. *Psychological Review,* 1969, *76*, 559–573.   (a)

Underwood, B. J. Some correlates of item repetition in free-recall learning. *Journal of Verbal Learning and Verbal Behavior,* 1969, *8*, 83–94.   (b)

Underwood, B. J. Individual differences as a crucible in theory construction. *American Psychologist,* 1975, *30*, 128–134.

Underwood, B. J., & Ekstrand, B. R. An analysis of some shortcomings in the interference theory of forgetting. *Psychological Review,* 1966, *73*, 540–549.

Underwood, B. J., & Ekstrand, B. R. Word frequency and cumulative proactive inhibition. *Journal of Experimental Psychology,* 1967, *74*, 193–198.

Underwood, B. J., & Ekstrand, B. R. Linguistic associations and retention. *Journal of Verbal Learning and Verbal Behavior,* 1968, *7*, 162–171.

Underwood, B. J., & Freund, J. S. Effect of temporal separation of two tasks on proactive inhibition. *Journal of Experimental Psychology,* 1968, *78*, 50–54.

Underwood, B. J., Kapelak, S. M., & Malmi, R. A. Integration of discrete verbal units in recognition memory. *Journal of Experimental Psychology: Human Learning and Memory,* 1976, *2*, 293–300.

Underwood, B. J., & Postman, L. Extraexperimental sources of interference in forgetting. *Psychological Review,* 1960, *67*, 73–95.

Underwood, B. J., & Schulz, R. W. *Meaningfulness and verbal learning.* Philadelphia: Lippincott, 1960.

Wells, J. E. Strength theory and judgments of recency and frequency. *Journal of Verbal Learning and Verbal Behavior,* 1974, *13*, 378–392.

Winograd, E. List differentiation, recall, and category similarity. *Journal of Experimental Psychology,* 1968, *78*, 510–515.   (a)

Winograd, E. Retention of list differentiation and word frequency. *Journal of Verbal Learning and Verbal Behavior,* 1968, *7*, 859–863.   (b)

Winograd, E. List differentiation as a function of frequency and retention interval. *Journal of Experimental Psychology Monograph Supplement,* 1968, *76*, (2, Pt. 2).   (c)

Wolff, P. Trace quality in the temporal ordering of events. *Perceptual and Motor Skills,* 1966, *22*, 283–286.

Zelkind, I., & Sprug, J. *Time Research: 1172 studies.* Metuchen, New Jersey: Scarecrow Press, 1974.

Zimmerman, J., & Underwood, B. J. Ordinal position knowledge within and across lists as a function of instructions in free-recall learning. *Journal of General Psychology,* 1968, *79*, 301–307.

Subject Index